CAMBRIDGE LIBRARY COLLECTION

Books of enduring scholarly value

History

The books reissued in this series include accounts of historical events and movements by eye-witnesses and contemporaries, as well as landmark studies that assembled significant source materials or developed new historiographical methods. The series includes work in social, political and military history on a wide range of periods and regions, giving modern scholars ready access to influential publications of the past.

The Crisis of the Sugar Colonies

Written as four public letters, this book condemns the intention by the French to reinstate older slavery practices on its colonies in the West Indies. James Stephen (1758–1832) was a lawyer who, after moving to St Kitts with his family to earn a living, became a supporter of the abolition movement. On his return to London in 1794, Stephen became involved with the anti-slavery group, the Clapham Sect, whose members included William Wilberforce, and with whom Stephen developed a lifelong friendship. Elected as a Member of Parliament in 1808, Stephen contributed to drafting legislation for slave registration on the island of Trinidad, which became a model for other slave colonies. Stephen believed that the reinstatement of older slavery practices on French colonies in the West Indies would lead to slave revolts, and have significant consequences for the neighbouring British colonies. This work was published in London in 1802.

T0381610

Cambridge University Press has long been a pioneer in the reissuing of out-of-print titles from its own backlist, producing digital reprints of books that are still sought after by scholars and students but could not be reprinted economically using traditional technology. The Cambridge Library Collection extends this activity to a wider range of books which are still of importance to researchers and professionals, either for the source material they contain, or as landmarks in the history of their academic discipline.

Drawing from the world-renowned collections in the Cambridge University Library, and guided by the advice of experts in each subject area, Cambridge University Press is using state-of-the-art scanning machines in its own Printing House to capture the content of each book selected for inclusion. The files are processed to give a consistently clear, crisp image, and the books finished to the high quality standard for which the Press is recognised around the world. The latest print-on-demand technology ensures that the books will remain available indefinitely, and that orders for single or multiple copies can quickly be supplied.

The Cambridge Library Collection will bring back to life books of enduring scholarly value (including out-of-copyright works originally issued by other publishers) across a wide range of disciplines in the humanities and social sciences and in science and technology.

The Crisis of
the Sugar Colonies

*Or, an Enquiry into the Objects
and Probable Effects of the French Expedition
to the West Indies*

JAMES STEPHEN

CAMBRIDGE
UNIVERSITY PRESS

CAMBRIDGE UNIVERSITY PRESS

Cambridge, New York, Melbourne, Madrid, Cape Town, Singapore,
São Paolo, Delhi, Dubai, Tokyo, Mexico City

Published in the United States of America by Cambridge University Press, New York

www.cambridge.org
Information on this title: www.cambridge.org/9781108020473

© in this compilation Cambridge University Press 2010

This edition first published 1802
This digitally printed version 2010

ISBN 978-1-108-02047-3 Paperback

THE CRISIS OF

THE

SUGAR COLONIES;

OR,

AN ENQUIRY

INTO THE

OBJECTS AND PROBABLE EFFECTS

OF THE

French Expedition

TO

THE WEST INDIES;

And their Connection with the

COLONIAL INTERESTS OF THE BRITISH EMPIRE.

TO WHICH ARE SUBJOINED,

SKETCHES OF A PLAN

FOR SETTLING THE

VACANT LANDS

OF

TRINIDADA.

IN FOUR LETTERS

TO THE

RIGHT HON. *HENRY ADDINGTON,*

CHANCELLOR OF THE EXCHEQUER, &c.

London:

PRINTED FOR J. HATCHARD,

Bookseller to Her Majesty, No. 190, (Opposite York House,) Piccadilly.

———••••••———

1802.

ADVERTISEMENT.

THAT the Reader may not suppose the general views of West India affairs which are disclosed in these sheets to have been suggested or influenced by the news lately received from St. Domingo, it may be proper to apprise him that three of the Letters, and great part of the fourth, were printed before the Public was possessed of any intelligence respecting the arrival of the French Expedition at that Island.

In fact this work was commenced very early in the year, and was nearly finished a month ago, though private avocations and other causes have till now unavoidably delayed its completion, and retarded its progress through the press.

March 27, 1802.

CONTENTS.

LETTER I.

LETTER II.

country and the climate.—Difficulties of keeping the negroes in subjection if conquered, and of restoring permanently the former system of bondage.

LETTER III.

The probable consequences of the expedition more immediately affecting the interest of Great Britain in the West Indies considered. —1st, Consequences of the total failure of the enterprise.—2d, Those of a middle event or compromise; or of an immediate agreement on the basis of the liberty of the negroes.—3d, Probable effects of the entire success of the supposed enterprise of the Republic.—Dangers to which the British Islands will in either of these cases be exposed.

LETTER IV.

*Measures that the prospects opened in the former letters should suggest.—A strict neutrality between France and her Colonies recommended.—Means of defence that ought to be prepared in our West India Islands.—Right of Parliament to make laws for the government of the Colonies considered.—*THOUGHTS ON THE MEANS OF SETTLING TRINIDADA.*— The vacant lands ought not to be settled by means of slavery and the Slave Trade.—The*
sale

TO THE

RIGHT HONOURABLE

HENRY ADDINGTON,

&c. &c.

───────◆───────

Sir,

A STRANGER solicits your attention on a subject of the highest importance; a subject which requires from you, as Prime Minister of this country, early and anxious investigation.

The voice of advice to a Minister when public, is generally hostile; but I am not an enemy, nor will my purpose be found unfriendly : indeed an Englishman can hardly, at this hour, be adverse to your administration, upon principles that fairly belong to a lover of his country. Your claims on the gratitude of the nation, are undeniably great. You gallantly took the helm at a moment of unparallelled danger, and already we have weathered the storm: The dawn of your administration has been a rapid passage

from

from danger to security, from famine to plenty, from arduous and seemingly interminable war to peace.

Nor is it essential to the glory of this contrast, to assert that the merit of the transition belongs exclusively to yourself. While we ascribe to the bounty of Providence, the late exuberant harvest, and to its supreme and over-ruling sway, the whole deliverance, and while in the next place we fairly allow to your predecessors much of what your own candour ascribed to them as to the concluding triumphs of our arms, it will not be forgotten that the judicious use of means and opportunities, by which advantages have been improved into blessings, has been all your own. Neither depressed by calamity, nor distracted by difficulties, nor inflated by success, you have displayed in the management of the helm of state a wisdom not inferior to the courage and disinterestedness with which it was assumed.

With such a minister, the admonitions of the press may not be necessary to add to the native force of truth the influence of its publicity; but the subject to which I would solicit your attention, is one upon which the public mind is not, I fear, sufficiently enlightened; and the popular voice, which is in some cases a salutary controul, may in others be a needful aid, to the measures of a wise administration.

of

Of the peace you have given to your country,
the conditions do honour to your judgement.
They have enlarged the bounds of the British
empire and to an extent full as great as was either
reasonable to expect, or prudent to require. Of the
French conquests in Europe it would have been
absurd to hope the restitution; and if there be
any man who still thinks a larger portion of our
own in distant parts of the globe ought to have
been retained, he forgets the nature of those dangers which the war was so long prosecuted to
avert, and to diminish which, as much as possible, was the British pacificator's most important
object. He does not sufficiently consider that in
the social, as in the natural body, extension is not
strength; and that still more widely to disperse
our much scattered energies, would have been to
lessen, rather than encrease, our security against a
rival force, formidable chiefly by its vicinity and
its concentration: nor do such politicians remember that commerce is the best sedative for the restless spirit of a warlike people; and their transmarine possessions the best guarantees of their pacific
engagements to the greatest of maritime states.

For my own part, I freely confess that, could
we have obtained the cession of all our colonial
conquests, I should have thought a Peace of
such splendid acquisition, far less advantageous
than the terms which your moderation has em-
braced.

Cessions

Cessions more extensive, could scarcely have been sincere; and would rather have resembled jewels lent to adorn a victim, than genuine offerings on the altar of Peace.

But, it is useless to add the applause of a single voice to that chorus of approbation raised by parliament, and the nation at large: Nor is it the object of this address to justify the wisdom of the treaty, or throw new light on its advantages; but rather to point out some serious dangers of which the peace, prudent and beneficial as it is, has unavoidably quickened the approach.

Already one of its consequences has strongly excited, and still fixes the public attention. No sooner were the ports of France released from the long embargo which our victorious and irresistible navy had imposed, than armaments of great magnitude began to be prepared in them; and with such dispatch were they compleated, that, in little more than two months from the ratification of the preliminary articles, a powerful expedition issued forth, consisting, according to general and uncontradicted report, of 25 sail of the line, and 25,000 regular troops.

That St. Domingo is the place of destination of this very formidable force, we have not only the warrant of uniform rumour, but, if I mistake not, of official authority for believing; but all beyond that point is uncertainty and anxious conjecture.

What

[5]

What specific changes the armament on its
arrival is to operate or attempt; and whether its
ultimate objects are safe or perilous, friendly or
hostile to this country, are questions not less
doubtful than important. Like the Trojans, who sallying from their
gates to enjoy their sudden and unhoped for
Peace, were soon arrested by the sight of the
stupendous horse, we gaze with wonder on
this great effort of our recent enemy, the post-
humous birth of war, and as in their case,

Scinditur incertum studia in contraria vulgus.

While many are loud in expressing their rash
approbation, and even exhort us to assist in
fixing this portentous force in the colonial cita-
del, others suspiciously exclaim

―― in nostros fabricata est machina muros ;
Inspectura domos, venturaque desuper urbi.

I hope, therefore, it will not be uninteresting,
and am sure it will not be unimportant, to enquire, as I propose to do in the following pages,
First.—*What are presumably the objects of
the French West India expedition?*
Secondly.—*What consequences interesting to
Great Britain are likely to result from it?*
Lastly.—*What measures does the probability
of such consequences demand from the prudence
of the* BRITISH *Government?*

In

In attempting to ascertain in the first place, the true objects of this grand enterprise of the Republic, I will dismiss from the field of conjecture, as too improbable to be seriously received, the notion of a design *directly* and *immediately* hostile to this country. Such barefaced perfidy would be too repugnant to the known policy of the Chief Consul, if not also to his principles, to be reasonably feared ; and it would be wronging your wisdom, Sir, and that of your colleagues in the Cabinet, to suppose that the expedition would have been allowed to sail unmolested, had you not been furnished with satisfactory evidence that his views were sincerely pacific.

As a necessary consequence of the same principles, I will presume that the French Colonies are the only theatre on which these armaments are designed immediately to act. " But what enemy is to be combated there, or what political ends accomplished by the power or terror of the sword?" Here again opinions are greatly divided.

While some persons speak of St. Domingo as a revolted colony, that, like the United States of America, has renounced its allegiance to the parent state, and is therefore to be reduced by force to its former dependence, others appear to view the quarrel as a mere contest for power between Toussaint and Buonaparte ; and

to

to imagine that the question lies between the Constitution lately framed by the former, and the military government of the latter; between the Consul of St. Domingo, and the Consul of France.

Politicans of a third class, comprising, I believe, almost all who are well informed of West India affairs, carry their views much farther, and conclude that the true, though unavowed, purpose of the French Government in this expedition, is to restore the old system of negro slavery in St. Domingo, and in the other colonies wherein it has been subverted.

The last of these opinions appears to me by far the most probable; and I purpose to offer some reasons in its support. It is, however, requisite previously to state, generally indeed, and briefly, yet not without precision, what the old system of slavery substantially was, and in what points its restitution will alter the present condition of the negroes.

Without some accurate preliminary knowledge of the difference between these two states, we cannot properly estimate the probability of the supposed design, nor the difficulties afterwards to be considered, that will attend its execution.

That the true nature of West India slavery is very imperfectly understood in this country, may appear a bold proposition; but is one, which,

which, from personal and long acquaintance with that system, and from ample opportunities of hearing the opinions prevalent in England on the subject, I am led with some confidence to affirm.

Neither the friends nor the enemies of the slave trade, seem to me to have attended sufficiently to that feature, which is in truth the most essential characteristic of colonial bondage, and chiefly distinguishes it from every other state of man, that is known to the traveller, or the historian.

" Are we then," it may be asked with alarm, " are we to have new facts disclosed ; and new " contradictions to decide upon between the " Abolitionists and the Planters?" By no means. The misapprehension I alledge, arises neither from the want nor the inconsistency of evidence ; but from inattention to facts perfectly notorious, and never controverted or denied.

That West India slaves, whether French or English, are the property of their master, and transferrable by him, like his inanimate effects ; that in general he is absolute arbiter of the extent and the mode of their labour, and of the quantum of subsistence to be given in return for it ; and that they are disciplined and punished at his discretion, direct privation of life or member excepted ; these are prominent
                                                            features,

features, and sufficiently known, of this state of slavery.

Nor is the manner in which the labour of slaves is conducted, a matter of less publicity. Every man who has heard any thing of West India affairs, is acquainted with the term negro-*drivers;* and knows, or may know, that the slaves in their ordinary field labour are *driven* to their work; and during their work, in the strict sense of the term, " driven," as used in Europe; though this statement no more involves an intimation, that in practice the lash is incessantly, or with any needless frequency, applied to their backs, than the phrase "to drive a team of horses," imports that the waggoner is continually smacking his whip. I use the comparison merely as descriptive, and not in censure of the West India system; with the accusation, or defence, of which, in a moral view, my argument, let it be observed, has no necessary connection. It is enough for my purpose, that in point of fact, no feature of West India slavery is better known, or less liable to controversy or doubt, than this established method in which field labour is enforced.

But a nearer and more particular view of this leading characteristic, may be necessary to those who have never seen a gang of negroes at their work. When employed in the labour of the field, as, for example, in *holeing a cane piece, i. e.*

in

in turning up the ground with hoes into paral-
lel trenches, for the reception of the cane plants,
the slaves, of both sexes, from twenty, perhaps, to
fourscore in number, are drawn out in a line, like
troops on a parade, each with a hoe in his hand,
and close to them in the rear is stationed, a driver,
or several drivers, in number duly proportioned
to that of the gang. Each of these drivers, who
are always the most active and vigorous negroes
on the estate, has in his hand, or coiled round
his neck, from which by extending the handle,
it can be disengaged in a moment, a long thick
and strongly plaited whip, called a *cart whip;*
the report of which is as loud, and the lash as
severe, as those of the whips in common
use with our waggoners, and which he has
authority to apply at the instant when his
eye perceives an occasion, without any pre-
vious warning.—Thus disposed, their work be-
gins, and continues without interruption for a
certain number of hours, during which, at the
peril of the drivers, an adequate portion of land
must be holed.

As the trenches are generally rectilinear, and
the whole line of holers advance together, it
is necessary that every hole or section of the
trench should be finished in equal time with the
rest; and if any one or more negroes were allowed to throw in the hoe with less rapidity or
energy than their companions in other parts of
the

the line, it is obvious that the work of the latter must be suspended; or else, such part of the trench as is passed over by the former, will be more imperfectly formed than the rest. It is, therefore, the business of the drivers, not only to urge forward the whole gang with sufficient speed, but sedulously to watch that all in the line, whether male or female, old or young, strong or feeble, work as nearly as possible in equal time, and with equal effect. The tardy stroke must be quickened, and the languid invigorated; and the whole line made to *dress*, in the military phrase, as it advances. No breathing time, no resting on the hoe, no pause of languor, to be repaid by brisker exertion on return to work, can be allowed to individuals: All must work, or pause together.

I have taken this species of work as the strongest example: But other labours of the plantation are conducted upon the same principle, and, as nearly as may be practicable, in the same manner.

When the nature of the work does not admit of the slaves being drawn up in a line abreast, they are disposed, when the measure is feasible, in some other regular order, for the facility of the drivers superintendence and coercion. In carrying the canes, for instance, from the field to the mill, they are marched in files, each with a bundle on his head, and with the driver in the rear : His

voice

voice quickens their pace, and his whip, when necessary, urges on those who attempt to deviate or loiter in their march.

Some parts indeed of the work of a plantation can only be done by the slaves in a state of dispersion, such as plucking the grass blade by blade in the ranges, or hedge rows, or on the mountains, for the provender of the horses and cattle. It is obvious that, in such cases, the immediate coercion of the driver cannot be applied; recourse is therefore had to the mode of individual task-work. Each slave, for example, is obliged to produce and deliver to the driver or overseer, within a limited time, a bundle of grass of a certain magnitude, on pain of immediate punishment by the cart-whip on his return from the field; and to quicken exertion at this task the time allowed for it is a part of the respite from more regular work, given to the slave, both for this purpose, and for preparing and eating his meal; so that if he wastes time in grass-hunting, he loses in the same proportion the comfort of his dinner, or perhaps the dinner itself, from want of time to prepare it. Yet so inadequate are these seemingly powerful expedients to supply *with men used to be driven*, the presence of the driver, that the bundles of grass are rarely brought in by all the slaves in due time, and of sufficient magnitude; and it has been observed of this part of

their

their work in the English Islands, that the neglect of it occasions more punishment than all the rest of their trespasses put together.

With these, and other necessary exceptions of solitary work, such as that performed by sugar-boilers and certain artificers, the compulsion of labour by the physical impulse or present terror of the whip is universal; and it would be as extraordinary a sight in a West India Island to see a line or file of negroes without a driver behind them, as it would be in England to meet a team of horses on a turnpike road without a carman or waggoner. Let me again profess, that the comparison is not made for the sake of odium, but only for illustration, which no less offensive image that occurs to me can so well furnish.

Such then, Sir, antecedently to the revolution, were the most important lineaments of the condition of the negroes in the French Colonies: unless it differed in these points, which, during many years residence in their neighbourhood I never heard asserted, from the state of the English slaves. *The negroes were the absolute, vendible property of the master, were worked and maintained at his discretion,* and were driven at their labours in the field.*

* The regulations of the *Code noir* which went partly to restrain the abuse of this power and that of punishment, were almost wholly neglected in practice.—See *Annales du Conseil Souverain de la Martinique.*—Tome i. 262-3, and 281.

A great

A great change has since been introduced at St. Domingo, Cayenne, and Guadaloupe; in the former by insurrection, in the two latter by decrees of the National Convention of France; and I would, in the next place, briefly enquire what have been its nature and effects.

Of the interior affairs of those Colonies since this change took place very little distinct information has been attainable in Europe. The press, which by giving domestic publicity to the events of a civilized community, brings them easily to the notice of its neighbours, has naturally been inactive among an illiterate people; and they have been visited only by persons whose errand was commerce or war, and who have in general had little desire, and less opportunity, to procure statistical intelligence; and as little disposition to lay such intelligence as they chanced to acquire before the public on their return.

The danger that might have attended research, in a country yet agitated by the waves of revolution, a country where a white face was an ensign of hostility, has doubtless tended powerfully to restrain curiosity in the visitors of St. Domingo.

But after full allowance made for all these obstacles, there will remain considerable ground for surprise at the profound darkness that hangs over some parts of this interesting subject. From the interior of St. Domingo in particular, scarcely one distinct ray has reached our horizon;

horizon, and its affairs are almost as unknown to Europe, as those of any nation in the centre of Africa,

——Res altâ rerrâ et caligine mersas.

Enough, however, has transpired, and enough may be clearly inferred from known political effects, to prove that the negro bondage, to the great characteristics of which I have called your attention, exists no more in those Colonies. The negroes are no longer the property of a master, transferable at his will; he is no longer the uncontrouled assessor of their labour, and of the returns to be given for it by himself; and by whatever sanctions public or private, industry may be enforced, the cultivators are certainly not worked as formerly, *under the lash of a driver.*

All the accounts, such as we have, which profess to give information of the new system, are thus far unanimous.

They generally also represent the negroes of St. Domingo, as living for the most part in great indolence; and agriculture, except so far as respects the easy culture of coffee and provisions, as being in a very languishing state; a description which pretty clearly imports the absence of the driver, and of the authority of private owners. Nor do such accounts admit of stronger confirmation than that
which

which arises from the state of the exports of that once flourishing colony; which though said of late to have greatly encreased, have since the Revolution, been insignificantly small when compared to their former extent.

From the regulations respecting field labour, published by Toussaint in October 1800, the same inferences, as to the new condition of the negroes, may undeniably be drawn; since for the purpose of enforcing industry, the fear of military punishments is in every case, made the substitute for the former coercion; and a labourer refusing to work, is, by these regulations, made liable to be *arrested*, and punished as a military deserter. But this punishment is not to be inflicted by the private master or by the drivers, who though they retain their name, are evidently disarmed of their whips, for the offenders are directed to be *carried before the military commandant, (see articles 2 and 7 of this curious ordinance in the Appendix.)*

From the smaller Island of Guadaloupe, and from Cayenne, our intelligence is rather more satisfactory and distinct. That these Colonies have by no means been left uncultivated there is a like uniformity of report; and the truth of it is proved by the considerable export trade which they maintained with neutral nations down to the end of the war; though there is great discordance between different accounts, as to the
quantity

quantity of their exported produce in comparison with its former amount. If a late report on
the colonies published by the French government may be credited, Cayenne, in an agricultural, as well as commercial view, never was
in a more flourishing state; and representations
equally favourable are given of Guadaloupe, by
persons who found their opinions on private
information respecting its exports to North
America. But these estimates are I doubt not,
greatly too large, especially in the latter case;
and it seems more probable that Gaudaloupe does
not at present produce one half, perhaps not much
more than one third, of its average crop of sugar
and coffee anterior to the revolution. To assign
reasons for this opinion would be a useless digression, for the fact is not material to my argument.

As it is notorious that in both the latter
colonies considerable quantities of produce are
raised, negro labour cannot be wholly disconti-
nued: But that this labour is obtained by other
means than the agency of the driver, is a fact
established by the agreement of every report,
public or private, direct or circuitous, with which
I am acquainted; and as I shall speedily shew,
is confirmed by still stronger and less resistible
evidence.

As the new state of the negroes both at Guadaloupe and Cayenne was introduced by the

c   government,

government, it was also defined by positive law, at the time of its introduction. You will find in the Appendix, a translation both of the conventional decree for enfranchising the slaves in the colonies, and of the proclamation with which was accompanied, when published by the French commissioners at Point Pitre in July 1794.

The negroes were by this law expressly released from slavery, and invested with all the rights of French citizens, and though industry was enjoined as a duty, the declared objects of that duty were themselves, their families, and the state, and not any particular master or employer. If it was intended that the new relations of stipendiary servant and master, should be formed between them and the same planters whose property they formerly had been, which does not clearly appear, the latter were at least required to give them a competent salary in return for their work.

In a word, they were placed, as far as an express law could place them, in the condition of English labourers; though perhaps obliged to work on a particular estate*.

From

---

* If reports prevalent in the Leeward Islands soon after this revolution were accurate, the limitation to a particular estate was the rule only in respect of such negroes as either could not or would

From the language of the French government *in* 1794, it would I admit be rash to infer its real and permanent designs. But Victor Hugues was not in a condition to violate with impunity his engagements to the negroes of Guadaloupe: By the sole aid of these newly-created citizens and soldiers, he was enabled to re-conquer that valuable colony; and solely by their fidelity and zeal could he hope to defend it during the war, against the unresisted masters of the seas. He was obliged therefore by political necessity to adhere to the promises on the faith of which they had joined him ; and that he did in good earnest establish and maintain their freedom was well known, to the terror of the British planters in all the adjacent islands.

It was, indeed but too manifestly proved by the astonishing effects which followed; especially in the disastrous æra of the insurrections in St. Vincent's and Grenada. The freedom of the negroes alone, and their zealous attachment to the government, not only made this little territory impregnable, but enabled Victor Hugues to pour from it, as from a volcano, terror and devastation around him.

would not employ themselves industriously upon some other plantation of their own choice. But the fact is not very material to my argument, and I wish not to overstate the extent of this revolution in any point, but rather where the case is doubtful, to lean to the other side.

That

That industry which the law enjoined, he found from causes shortly to be noticed, not easy to be enforced. In a great degree, he was probably obliged to acquiesce in the neg-lect of it; and if reports spread in the neigh-bouring British colonies in 1795 deserve cre-dit, he did not btain the degree of agricul-tural labour that was yielded in the infancy of his new system without resorting to the utmost severities of military discipline, treating the incorrigibly idle as mutineers, and punish-ing some of them with death, as examples to the rest.

Such reports are however liable to much suspi-cion; for never certainly were there sronger po-pular motives to blacken the character of an ene-my, than those which prompted the tongue of fame at that period against Victor Hugues, and his system of government, among his West In-dian neighbours.

I do not wish to be his apologist, for he seems to have been a ferocious and unprincipled cha-racter; but it is unlikely that his black troops would contentedly be the instruments of such se-verity on their brethren; and there is no satis-factory evidence of any such executions.

The fact however if it existed, proves the truth of my proposition : for if recourse was had to such severe measures, they were acts of *public*, not of *private*, authority, and were substitutes
for

for the power of the master, and the coercion of
the driver's lash.

At the same time, the prevalence of such a rumour whether true or false in the neighbouring
islands, some of which lie within sight of the
shores of Guadaloupe, evinces that the general
change in the condition of the French negroes
was there notorious. It was the indolence produced by that change that was supposed to
have demanded, or from the brutality of Hugues
to have received, so rigorous a species of correction.

From the silence of report as to opposite facts,
an inference still more convincing may be drawn.
It never has been alleged to my knowledge,
and during eight years which have elapsed since
the express enfranchisement in question my
attention has been alive to the subject, it has
never been the topic of rumour public or private,
that negroes have been seen at Guadaloupe or
Cayenne, working under the whip of the driver.

This in its nature is not a fact which if
it existed could escape observation. By thousands of Americans and other neutral persons
resorting to those colonies, and by very many
British who have been carried thither as pri-
soners of war, negroes must have been often
seen at work; and even from the decks of the
British and other vessels coasting along the
shore or Guadaloupe, they must frequently have
been

been observed, had they worked in gangs as formerly, with the drivers very distinguishable in the rear.

Is it then to be imagined that a fact so decisive of the re-establishment or continuance of the old system, would not have been announced in our Islands, and from thence to the British public? Surely Sir, I need not remind you how large a stake our West India fellow subjects have, or think they have, in the public opinions on these matters; or ask you to reflect how much and how naturally the example of the revolutions in the French Islands excited their alarms! A moment's consideration therefore will convince you, that the total failure of an experiment the final success of which must be at once dangerous and opprobrious to the system they fondly support, would have been eagerly and triumphantly announced: nor could the obvious policy have been overlooked of trumpeting in the ears of the English negroes the restoration of the cart-whip at Guadaloupe.

To my mind, this negative argument is a stronger proof than the testimony of a hundred witnesses of what I am warranted by the result of much private enquiry to believe, that a negro driver is no longer to be seen in these colonies.

Of positive details even respecting the new system, we are not wholly unprovided.

The

The return to be made to the negroes of a
plantation collectively for their annual labour,
was fixed by Victor Hugues at one-third of
the value of the produce. This was also the
general law at Cayenne, and, if I rightly remember, at St. Domingo; though laws have
scarcely had any operation in that distracted
Island. Another third was allotted to the owner;
and the rest to the Republic.

According to other accounts, the remaining
third was to supply the expences of the estate;
which seems the most probable, because without
a provision for these, the owner's share would
have been exhausted in sustaining them, and
the share of the Republic would have been too
palpably enormous. But, perhaps, the contradic-
iction may be explained by the fact, that both
at Guadaloupe and St. Domingo, a great proportion of the estates were by forfeiture or seques-
tration, in the hands of the government.

Nothing obviously could be more inconve-
nient, than so precarious and distant a remune-
ration for labour as a share of a West India
crop, to men who must live by their daily labour: it was, therefore, speedily improved by
Victor Hugues, into an allowance, either by
way of commutation or advance, payable pe-
riodically to each labourer; and this he origiu-
ally fixed at such a number of livres per week,
as considering the great scarcity of specie in the
colony,

colony, was a tolerably ample subsistence, I think it was nine livres.

As far as private enquiry has enabled me to form a judgment of the fact, the rate of wages both there and at Cayenne has since been fixed from time to time by the Government; which has also exercised an intimate superintendance and controul both over the masters and the plantation negroes, obliging the latter to labour, as well as the former to give what is deemed a sufficient support.

The *regime* by which these ends are accomplished, is wholly military; and refractoriness in the negroes is punished when necessary, not by the master, or at his discretion, but by the order of a public officer or court.

That authoritative information on these points cannot be obtained, is much to be regretted. I might appeal, however to proclamations of the executive authority at Guadaloupe, and those of Toussaint, as well as of the Commissioners and agents of the French Government at St. Domingo, in further proof, that industry however regulated, is now considered as a duty to be inculcated by persuasion, or enforced by the sanctions of municipal law aided by a military police, and not a mere physical effect to be excited by the application of the lash.

I allude here to papers with which you, Sir, and every reader must be familiar, as they have often

often been published in our daily prints. They contain strong expostulations against the vice of indolence, and earnest invitations to agricultural industry, as essential both to public and private happiness. Now such addresses from the governors to the governed, do not more clearly prove indolence to be a prevalent bad habit in the community, than they demonstrate the total subversion of the old system in all its fundamental parts. Such a proclamation if addressed to the negroes in an English West India Island, could only be considered as an impertinent interference with the authority of the master, and the interior discipline of his plantation; as a reflection on the activity of the drivers, and a cruel mockery of the slaves.

Perhaps Sir, you may think that I am pressing this point with more assiduity than it requires. To the well informed in West India affairs, it is certainly unnecessary to prove the true nature of the revolutions in question : but a great majority of the public, being ignorant as I have already observed, of the distinguishing character of negro-bondage, is of course liable to much imposition and mistake in judging of those revolutions by which that bondage has been abolished, and of the important changes which have been produced : and advantage has been taken of this circumstance to propagate

in

in the public mind errors which may be of dangerous consequence.

It is curious enough to observe in how loose and unintelligent a manner, persons even of general political knowledge, will express themselves on this subject. Since the recent insurrection in Guadaloupe for instance, it has been often said in the best conducted public prints, that the negroes had " declared *for freedom :*" that " they had demanded their liberty from " their masters ;" &c. and it has been called " a revolt of the slaves."

That the cause of that remarkable insurrection was an attempt of Lacrosse under the orders of Buonapaite, to restore the old system of slavery, I shall hereafter offer some reasons for believing: But it is singular, that *in the year* 1802, the slavery of the negroes of that Island should be spoken of in London newspapers as a state from which they had never emerged, and the chains of which they were newly attempting to break.

Unhappily in this, as in other cases, the ambiguity of language is fatal to the cause of truth. The great and recent abuses of the terms, " liberty and freedom," " slavery and bond- " age," have given them a meaning in European ears widely different from their genuine political import; but infinitely more distant still
from

from what they are practically felt to imply in the West Indies. There are no proper and peculiar names to distinguish the state of the negro in bondage, from his enfranchised condition. We, therefore call him in the one state a *slave*; in the other, a *freeman;* and the European is not aware that the distinction has no similitude to those which have occasioned so many important, and so many foolish quarrels, in his own quarter of the globe; that it has no affinity with aristocracy on the one hand, or with democracy on the other; with Jacobinism, or with Anti-jacobinism; that it immeasurably transcends in its importance to the individual, the most extreme differences known in Europe, in the degrees of municipal freedom or restraint between the most favoured, and least fortunate people; between the peasant of England, and the peasant of Russia; that it is in truth, little short of the whole difference between brutal and rational nature.

Hence the necessity of fixing, if I was able, with precision, the true nature of that condition inadequately defined by the term *slavery* from which the French negroes have passed, and its essential difference from that to which they have attained.

Having accomplished I trust that preliminary task, as far as consists with the plan and the necessary limits of this address, I proceed

to

to offer my reasons for suspecting that *a counter-revolution in the state of the enfranchised
negroes, is the main object of France in her
West India expedition.*

The great and urgent motive by which the
counsels of the Republic may be presumed to
be prompted in regard to the West Indies, is an
impatient wish to restore the agricultural and
commercial value of her colonies.

The monoply of the European sugar markets
by her great rival, is a disadvantage not patiently to be borne. The restoration of her marine too
in point of comparative importance cannot be
hoped for, while a nursery so great as West India
navigation, is nearly lost to her, and possessed
almost exclusively by Great Britain. Nor does
her revenue, less than her maritime interests,
demand the recovery of her colonial resources
in all their former magnitude.

But in the sugar colonies of France, especially in that whose former importance eclipsed all the rest united, and the extent of which
has been vastly increased by the cession of
Spanish St. Domingo, *negro liberty* seems to
be an insuperable obstacle to all these great and
necessary views.

While the negroes were in bondage, that colony was rich and flourishing by the effects of
their labour; since their enfranchisement, it has
become

become comparatively almost a neglected waste. All the solicitations of the officers of the Republic, all the influence and authority of their own favorite Chiefs, have failed to recall them to any tolerabie degree of regular industry. What then remains, but either to restore the rigid yoke of the private master, and renew the coercion of the cart-whip, or permanently to leave this fine Island in its present unprofitable state?

Thus it appears at first sight not nnnatural for the Chief Consul to reason. Perhaps, indeed it may appear in the sequel that such a counter-revolution will not easily be effected; and that if effected, it would not durably restore the prosperity of the Colony. But this if not the surest, is at least the shortest, course: the necessities of the republic are urgent, and nations, as well as individuals,

—" Often strike their dearest wish far off,
Through ardor to possess it.————

Besides, it is not consonant with the character of the Chief Consul to be deterred by difficulties : he delights in a rapid dazzling atchievement: the tardy triumphs of a cautious policy, are not congenial to his temper, and may arrive too late to consolidate his power, or to feast his appetite for fame.

Numerous

Numerous and powerful private interests too
may probably concur with his own, and the apparent interests of the republic, in demanding
from Buonaparte the re-establishment of the
former system.

The planters of the French Islands were not
only a very numerous and opulent body antecedently to the revolution, but so many of them
had been ennobled, and so many of the ancient
noblesse had either acquired estates in the Colonies, or intermarried with the families of opulent Creoles, that they possessed among the
highest orders, as well as in the commercial cir-
cles, a very extensive influence.

Their power and interest have no doubt been
in great measure lost by the general ruin of
their fortunes; very few of them, except at
Cayenne, and in the Islands conquered by Great
Britain, having escaped confiscation and exile.

Their counter-revolutionary principles, must
also, have contributed previously to the government of Buonaparte, to destroy their weight in
the republic. But the conciliatory system of the
Chief Consul has recalled from exile a great
part of this unfortunate body, who, as far as
can be collected, are friendly to his authority,
and he, if not partial to them as a particular
description of royalists, is at least disposed to
protect and favor them as a branch of that numerous party. If report may be credited, he is
even

even connected with them by marriage, Madam Buonaparte being as it is said, of a Creole family, and intitled to a plantation in one of the French Windward Islands.

The desire of conciliating a body of men, powerful by their numbers and connections, and formidable to a new government even by the desperate circumstances to which they are reduced, may concur with other and more generous motives to engage the Chief Consul in the enterprise of reinstating the planters in their estates.

But how can this work be accomplished consistently with the freedom of the negroes? To give back the land, without the means of its cultivation, would be a mockery, rather than a benefit. Are then the former slaves, and their issue born or grown up to puberty during ten years that have succeeded the Revolution, to be sent back to the plantations to which they formerly belonged, and obliged to work thereon as free labourers without the presence of the drivers.?

I shall presently have occasion to shew the formidable difficulties, of reducing such a project into practice. But let us suppose it accomplished, and enquire how it would affect the master.

Between him and these unwilling servants, mutual distrust and hatred would, in most cases to a high degree prevail. They have driven him

into

into exile, and laid waste his property perhaps
have shed the blood of some of his dearest relatives, during the horrors of the Revolution;
and though to the satisfactory renewal of any
intimate civil connection whatever between
them these are serious obstacles, they are
peculiarly adverse to the forming a relation
hitherto untried, to the success of which reci-
procal confidence and goodwill would be pecu
liarly requisite.

The stern system that was overthrown asked
for no such confidence; appealed to no feelings
of the heart for its security; but was perfectly
compatible with mutual distrust and detestation.
If therefore this sytem could be renewed, and
the authority of the drivers sustained against the
new character of the negroes by the energies of
the state, the master might again hope to sleep
in safety on his plantation, and carry on its business with effect. But I doubt whether a single
individual could be found among the exiled
planters, hardy enough to be desirous of regain-
ing his property at the peril of residing among
his former slaves, and holding the loosened
reins of such private authority as might be found
compatible with their freedom.

I here suppose the negroes to be obliged to labour exclusively for the former owner, or upon
the estate to which they formerly belonged,
like the *Adscripti Glebæ,* in many ancient and

even

even modern countries, and the *manorial villains* among our ancestors in this island. But were it proposed to leave them at freedom to choose their master, and the master to choose from the common stock the labourers he would employ, though tl e preceding objections would indeed be in some points lessened, other and more formidable difficulties would arise.

The planter's fortune and credit would in that case be irrecoverably impaired to the extent at least of the full value of the negroes once belonging to him, in whom he would no longer possess any species of property; and it would be left to depend on his success in the competition for servants, whether his plantation could immediately be brought into culture or not.

Credit was necessary to him even in his former flourishing circumstances; but where could he obtain it now? A merchant would perhaps, not be very prompt on any terms to embark his capital, on an ocean hitherto unexplored, with a view to the precarious returns to be expected from the labour of free negroes : But if the owner of a plantation has for ever lost the value of his slaves, his property is diminished by this reduction one third in its value, over and above all other losses and deteriorations by revolution and war. In receiving back the land despoiled of its works and buildings, and of all the stock necessary for its culture, without any renewed

D   property

property in the negroes, it would be a high estimate to say that he would be re-instated in two fifths of his former fortune; and let those who know the ordinary circumstances of West India estates, determine what relief planters in general would derive from such a partial restitution! Unless their former situations were widely different indeed from that of their English brethren, the Consul by such an act of justice might confer indeed some benefit on the unfortunate creditors or mortgagees, but certainly none at all on the planter himself.

How then in this case could new credit be obtained? or how without credit are the works to be rebuilt, and all the stock and costly implements to be supplied? Destitute of these, a sugar plantation would be like the cup of Tantalus to its unfortunate owner.

It seems probable for these and other reasons, that with all the difficulty of the attempt to re-establish the master's property in his negroes, and absolute authority over them, nothing less will satisfy the West Indian party in France. However hazardous the game, it is the only one that the Creole proprietor can play, with a chance of redeeming for his own benefit any part of the stake.

If we attend to the language and conduct of the Chief Consul, since peace with this country put him in a situation to attempt to regulate the
transmarine

transmarine interests of France, we shall find no
reason to disbelieve that these considerations
have had a decisive influence on his counsels.

In an elaborate report upon the situation of the
republic, presented by him to the legislative
body, and published in the Moniteur of Novem-
ber 24th, he thus expresses himself respecting
the West India colonies: " *In the West, Gua-*
" *daloupe has preserved a share of its agricul-*
" *ture and prosperity, &c.   In St. Domingo,*
" *some irregular acts have excited fears, &c.*
" *In these two islands there are no more slaves;*
" *all* ARE FREE; AND SO THEY SHALL REMAIN.
" *In Martinique, a different policy has been*
" *pursued: the practice of* SLAVERY HAS BEEN
" THERE CONTINUED, AND IT MUST BE PRE-
" SERVED. *It would cost too much to humanity,*
" *to attempt there a new revolution.   Guyana,*
" *and the Isles of France and of Reunion, have*
" *been faithful to the Republic, and have pros-*
" *pered, though under feeble, and uncertain ad-*
" *ministrations.*"

If any man can read this language, and retain
a doubt whether Buonaparte's views are inimical
or not to negro freedom, let him recollect that
Guadaloupe and St. Domingo were colonies
in which the avowal of such an enmity would
have united all hearts and hands in opposition to
the arms of the Republic, at that critical moment when the armaments were just departing
from

from her harbours; and that respecting Martinique there could be no motive for dissimulation in either case, because Great Britain was
bound to restore that island peaceably to his
possession and authority. The French planters
could certainly not offer a moment's opposition
to whatever measures the Consular government
might think fit to adopt, especially if such measures were of a nature popular among the slaves.

But if the Consul was sincere in his language
as to this island; what principle, moral or political, can make the sincerity of his promise to
the negroes of Guadaloupe worthy of a moment's credit?

To maintain two such opposite systems in
islands within sight of each other, would be not
more preposterous than impracticable. The pretence seems almost too gross for the blunt intel-
lects of the poor beings whom it was intended
to cajole.

But the emphatic silence as to the system intended for *Cayenne* or *Guyana,* makes the hypocrisy of this paper still more flagrant.

It is notorious that the negroes of that colony were in the same free condition with that
of their brethren in Guadaloupe; and that their
enfranchisement had been repaid by fidelity to
the Republic the Consul himself acknowledges.
In fact their freedom alone could have averted
the conquering arms of Great Britain; for an
expedition

expedition was actually meditating against the settlement, when the decree of enfranchisement arrived and made it impregnable.

That the colony has prospered under the new order of things this state paper also admits. *Yet no engagement is made to maintain negro liberty in Guyana:* on the contrary, it is spoken of in the same breath, and in the same manner, with the Isles of France and Bourbon, or Reunion, where the condition of the slaves has never been altered.

If it be asked why the same dissimulation was not necessary in regard to Cayenne as is supposed to have been practised towards the two other colonies, I answer, because it contained at the time of its revolution only about 15,000 slaves; while Guadaloupe had 100,000, and St. Domingo half a million*.

There

* By an official return made to the National Assembly of France, in 1790 St Domingo contained 480,000 slaves, and 24,848 free people of colour. In the same year 34,840 African slaves were imported. When, therefore, we add the further imports prior to the Revolution, and the many thousands of Guinea negroes captured in British slave-ships, and carried into the ports of that island during the war, we may after much allowance for the ravages of the sword, and without reckoning on any extraordinary increase by births, from the effects of the new system, or including the negroes of Spanish St. Domingo, reasonably suppose the island now to contain 500,000 negroes or persons of negro extraction. In
estimating

There was perhaps some further security against resistance in this case; for if a recent publication of the French government deserves credit, it would seem that Victor Hugues, the able and versatile agent of France, must have already effected at Cayenne some changes favourable to the restitution of the old system; but if so, his work will probably not be permanent*.

Were the nature and causes of the recent revolution in Guadaloupe fairly before the public, the Chief Consul's West India policy would perhaps be more clearly disclosed.

All we know of that remarkable event warrants the suspicion that *Lacrosse,* a governor lately sent from France, had attempted changes hostile to the freedom of the negroes. He arrived at Guadaloupe in the month of June last, with two frigates, and about 600 veteran troops;

estimating the number of negroes enfranchised by the Revolution, at *Guadaloupe,* I include the negroes of the small dependent Islands of Marigalante and the Saintes, and believe the estimate is too low.

* The paper alluded to neatly insinuates that the African slave trade had actually been restored in Guyana, by speaking of the imports of negroes as a proof of the growing prosperity of the Colony, but without directly noticing any change of system by which the trade had been legally revived. It is very observable, however, that though Victor Hugues's dispatches are referred to for this and other important particulars, no copy or extract from those dispatches is published.

and

and immediately set on foot interior changes, of which a known immediate effect was that of inducing many planters who were in exile in the neighbouring islands to return to their estates.

What those changes specifically were, he and the French Government have not thought proper to inform the European world. But dispatches and proclamations of this governor officially published in France in October last imported that he was introducing some important novelties in the interior administration; and though the true nature of these was veiled in obscure generalities, it was evident enough, that to enforce greater industry in the lower orders, and to draw tighter the cords of authority over them, were main objects of the projected reformation.

It was therefore very remarkable that *no salvo in favour of freedom,* nor any *protest against the restitution of the former bondage,* was to be found in these papers. The evident liability to suspicion in those points of all such acts of government in the free-negro colonies, had made the most solemn protestations of adherence to the principle of freedom invariable accompaniments of every former law and proclamation on like subjects; but on this occasion they were wholly omitted.

When with so striking a circumstance we
connect

connect the speedy event, we shall have little difficulty to determine the general character of Lacrosse's improvements. Within two months after his arrival there was a dangerous insurrection against him; and though he alledged in his dispatches, published in the Moniteur of December 3, that the commotion was speedily stifled, snd that he could answer for the tranquillity of the Colony, it was before the end of that month known in this country that he had been driven from his government, and all the white inhabitants at the same time expelled or imprisoned.

This Colony for eight years of war preceding his arrival had been faithful to the Republic, and undisturbed by civil commotions : innovations the most extreme that ever changed the civil destiny of man had not materially disturbed its internal peace : the negroes had submitted implicitly to successive governors ; and had even seen the popular founder of their freedom Victor Hugues, seized in their port by stratagem and sent a prisoner to France, by the authority of the Republic, yet were obedient and loyal to his successor. But Lacrosse's unknown measures, urged them at once into a general and successful rebellion ; and by the latest accounts they continued to set at defiance the authority of France, notwithstanding the knowledge that the sea was now open to her arms.

These

These facts Sir, are impressive, and I request your close attention to them.

They not only serve to paint the true views of Buonaparte in the West, but indicate pretty clearly what measure of resistance awaits him. To all these indications of a general design adverse to the freedom of the negroes, may be added the magnitude of the armament itself. That the sending out 25 sail of the line, and 25,000 troops, merely to extort from Toussaint a submission which he had not yet refused to the authority of the Republic, was an effort disproportionate to such an object, cannot well be denied ; and let it be remembered that when this great armament was dispatched from France, Guadaloupe was supposed to be in a state of tranquil submission to the Mother Country*.

I do not with some persons suspect that the designs of Buonaparte in this expedition are treacherous and hostile to Great Britain ; but it is because I conclude that he has in view an enterprize much more extensive and arduous than to obtain the recognition of his authority from Toussaint.

* Various accounts have lately been published, on what authority I know not, of very considerable further armaments having been recently dispatched to the West Indies from the ports of France, aud those of her allies or dependants.

As

As far then as the intentions of France can be inferred from the various indications which have been noticed, conjecture is uniformly guided to the same point, *a design to restore in St. Domingo, Guadaloupe, and Cayenne, the old species of bondage.* That this is her true aim has been shewn to be probable, from the inevitable tardiness of any other expedient to restore her colonial agriculture, and from the repugnance of delay as well to the genius of the Consul, as to the pressing exigencies of the state. It has been shewn to be probable also, from the interests and unquestionable wishes of a large and powerful body of men in the Republic whom Buonaparte must be desirous to conciliate; and the probability appears to be greatly strengthened, by the language he has publicly used, by the measures of his chosen governors in the West Indies, and by the magnitude of those military preparations the object of which I have attempted to explore.

I am, &c. &c.

LETTER

LETTER II.

———

Sir,

I proposed in the se-
cond place to enquire, *what consequences interesting to Great Britain are likely to result
from the depending West India enterprise of
the Republic?*

In the course of that enquiry, to which we
now proceed, the justice of those important
views which it is my wish to unfold, will not
be found entirely to depend on the truth of the
conclusion which it was attempted in the preceding letter to establish.

For the purpose of determining more clearly
the most probable immediate effects of the expedition, I shall indeed assume in the first place,
that its object is such as has been inferred; but
shall afterwards consider the result of a contrary
hypothesis; and shall reason to no ultimate or
prac-

practical conclusions, but such as will be found fairly to arise from the premises already laid down, or remaining to be adduced, if those premises were true in point of fact, whatever may be at this period the real designs of the Chief Consul.

This branch of the subject naturally resolves itself into two distinct, though closely allied, considerations.

FIRST. *The probable issue of the Expedition in the French Colonies.* SECONDLY. *The effects its success or failure are likely to produce in the British West India Islands.*

Within a very short period, probably before these sheets which I am now penning can issue from the press, the arrival and the first effects of the armament in question will be known in Europe.

They will probably be represented in the most favourable colours; and it is most likely that without the aid of exaggeration, they will be such as to give apparently a strong assurance of ultimate success. The towns and forts on the coast of St. Domingo will probably be conquered with great facility; perhaps, will offer no resistance; especially if the fleet and army should not be divided or retarded in their progress after their arrival at the Windward Islands, by necessary operations against Guadaloupe.

Appear-

Appearances still more promising may possibly mark the dawn of this interesting enterprise. Toussaint may submit; or if not, it will be an easy game for the Generals of the French army to avail themselves of the discord said already to prevail among the negroes of that Colony, or to scatter the seeds of new dissentions, so as to gain over some of their most powerful leaders, and considerable bodies of their troops. It is possible even, that by specious promises of a well regulated freedom a general submission to the authority of the Republic may be speedily obtained; and thus the whole work may appear to be at once accomplished.

And may not this success be real and permanent, as well as speedy? Certainly it may, if the views of the French Government ended here, and nothing more were desired than the political subordination of the colony to the parent state. But if the submission of the negroes be only, as I conclude, an object preliminary to the more arduous task of restoring the former bondage, the work after all the successes here supposed, will barely have commenced. The new foundation even will not have been firmly laid, when to the European eye the whole edifice may appear to be re-built.

It is when the true design shall be avowed, or begin to unfold itself: when the negroes shall discover, that not to the fasces of the Consul only, but to the whip of the driver, their submission

mission is demanded; when the master shall
take possession of his estate, and the bell and
the loud report of the drivers' whip, announcing
the approach of dawn, shall summon them again
to the field; it is then, that the arduous nature
of the undertaking will be felt; and that the
Republic will find like Great Britain, the difference between subduing the coast, and ruling
the interior, of this extensive Island; between
gaining the chiefs, and coercing the new formed people.

To estimate more clearly the practicability
of the supposed design, let us consider briefly,
first, the *motives*, and next, the *means* of resistance.

That on a state of bondage such as has been
here generally described the enfranchised slave
must cast his eye back with aversion and horror,
cannot be doubted. We may be apt to place upon
the distinctions of political freedom or restraint
known in Europe, more than a reasonable value;
but they shrink to nothing, when compared
with the unspeakable difference between the
terms " slave and free," in the colonies.

If men think the limitation of Royal Prero-
gative, worth the miseries and the blood, which
its defence has sometimes cost, when according to the poet,

" Of all the ills the human race endure,
" How small a part that kings can cause or cure !"

What

What energies are not likely to be called forth, what desperate struggles to be made, in defending not only private property, but the very capacity of possessing it; in defending a man's title to his own muscles and sinews; in maintaining the common privileges not merely of social, but of rational nature ! !

Is it objected, " They have once submit-" ted without resistance to such bondage, and " why not again?" I answer, it was antecedent to their experience of the yoke, and of the possibility of breaking it.

They were trained to the state from infancy without knowledge of a better; or were " *sea-*" *soned* to it, as the term is, when dejected and helpless exiles, in a land of novelty and wonder; when every feature of authority was armed by superstitious terrors, and the general reverential submission of all the fellow bondsmen among whom they were placed, contagiously strengthened their awe of the superior being whom they were taught to call *master.* Yet even in this " seasoning," many perished by the resistance of nature to the yoke; and not a few eluded it by suicide.

Renovation of this bondage after enfranchisement from it, is a work the practicability of which remains to be proved by experience; for by the laws of the West Indies the manumitted negro cannot forfeit his freedom.

The

The case of the runaway slave, could be the only subject of such an experiment; and as to him, it is proverbial that he is never reclaimed. When once hardy enough to have deserted from the field and breathed the air of liberty on the mountains, neither famine, nor perpetual perils in his fugitive state, nor the severe punishments which infallibly follow his apprehension, can deter him from relapsing into the same offence.— The disease is incurable; and the master, after trying all means, harsh or lenient, in vain, is generally glad to sell him for less than the half of his former value.

Among the various powerful feelings that will combine to inspire a large community of negroes inured by a ten years experience to the habits of freedom, with an aversion perfectly irreconcileable to their former state, there is one which claims particular attention.—It is one which will probably occasion much obstinacy in the attempt to refix their fetters, while it creates at least an equal pertinacity of resistance; I mean that antipathy to their former agricultural labours, which has already been so visible in the negroes of St. Domingo.

Man is naturally indolent, and impatient of bodily restraint. Though spurred by his hopes and fears into activity, and often to the most ardent exertions, he is with difficulty bent to the yoke of uniform and persevering labour.

The

The suggestions of foresight however are
very powerful impulses, especially when second-
ed by habit; and the Great Author of our na-
tures has conferred on them a mild, as well as
a rightful dominion. When we bow to the gold-
en sceptre of reason, obedience has many facilities, and its pains many mitigations. Nature
is not thwarted more rudely than the rational
purpose demands; and the mind, while it urges
on the material frame, cheers it in return with
refreshing and invigorating cordials.

Look at the most laborious peasant in Europe,
and if you please, the most oppressed : he is
toiling it is true from painful necessity; but it
is necessity of a moral kind, acting upon his rational nature ; and from which brutal coercion
differs as widely, as a nauseous drench in the
mouth of an infant, from the medicated milk
of its mother.

Is the impelling motive, fear of want, or dread
of a master's displeasure ; yet he sees on the
other hand, the approbation and reward attainable by exertions, whereof the degree at least
is for the moment spontaneous. Self-compla-
cency alleviates his toil, and hope presents to
his view, the hearty well-earned meal, the evening fire-side, and perhaps the gratifications of
the husband, or the father, in promoting the
well-being of those dearest to his heart. Is his
work fatiguing; he is at liberty at least, to

E   intro-

introduce some little varieties in the mode, or breaks in the continuity of it, which give him sensible relief. He can rest on his spade, or stay the plough a moment in the furrow; can gaze at a passing object, or stop a brother villager to spend a brief interval in talk.

To the reflecting mind, these little privileges will not appear unimportant, when contrasted with the hard and cheerless lot of the field negro. He, is not at liberty to relax his tired muscles, or beguile his weariness, either by voluntary pauses in labour, or by varying its mode: he must work on with his fellow slaves, let fatigue or satiety groan ever so much for a moment's respite, till the driver allows a halt.

But far more deplorable is the want of all those animating hopes that sweeten the toil of the European peasant. To the negro slave driven to his work, his involuntary exertions as they can plead no merit, can promise in general no reward. His meal will not be more plentiful, nor his cottage better furnished, by the fruits of his utmost toil. As to his wife and children, they can hardly be called his own: whether the property of the same, or a different owner, it is upon the master, not on himself, that their subsistence and well being depend.

The negro therefore casts his hoe from no impulse but that of fear, and fear brought so closely and continually into contact with its object, that

that we can hardly allow it to rise above brutal instinct, and call it rational foresight, without ascribing to the docility of the horse an equal elevation. The other great and pleasing spring of human action, hope, is entirely cut off.

When these peculiar circumstances are duly considered, the rooted aversion of the free negro to his former labours, cannot excite surprise. It is unnecessary to suppose that they were excessive in degree, for in their kind, they were too irksome to be by the most patient of our race contentedly endured, or remembered without abhorrence.

Neither is it necessary to suppose that the impending lash was in the ordinary routine of field duty often actually inflicted. The human team might when well broken, move on so regularly, as to make the whip in the hand of a humane driver little more than a mere ensign of authority; yet the sense of perpetual constraint, and ever goading necessity, would be much the same. The motive would still be instant fear though producing from habit a regular and equable movement.

It might be admitted even without danger to the argument, though I am sorry to say not without doing violence to truth, as well as probability, that this coarse actuation of the physical powers of the human frame by an external mind interested in their effect, was in general not pushed to excess; but was an impulse as leniently

and

and wisely regulated, as that of reason, when guided by the sympathies of the soul with the body to which nature has allied it.

Nay we might overlook the inevitable frequency of such excesses as masters of narrow or unfeeling minds, may be expected to practise; and suppose that in the time or measure of work, avarice armed with unlimited power, never exacted too much, nor ever made too little allowance for occasional or particular weakness; in other words, that while thrones in Europe too rarely find possessors fit to govern, the sceptre of a plantation falls into the hands of none but Antonines and Trajans!! Still we should see in this manner of enforcing work, and in the general circumstances of West India bondage, enough to account for a strong antipathy in the breast of the enfranchised negro to his former state, and its attendant labours.

If industry be not seldom wanting even among the lower classes in Europe; how can these poor husbandmen, who know the duty only by its thorns, be expected to practice it? My surprize I own is rather that with all the aid of military organization, in the hands of a government popular by giving freedom, agriculture has been in any degree kept up at Guadaloupe, and Cayenne, than that it has so greatly languished at St. Domingo.

Should it be objected, that this dislike to labour in their new state, is but a *prejudice,* which the they have had time to conquer, by observing the ease and the happy effects of voluntary industry; it may be answered, that victory over prejudice, especially in illiterate minds, is not soon or easily gained. Men far more advanced than negroes in the exercise of their reasoning powers, find it hard to abstract the essential nature of any subject of experience, from its usual, though adventitious attendants. We are not easily persuaded that a medical draught is not nauseous, and the pardoned convict would probably shudder at revisiting his dungeon, though for a purpose of curiosity or enjoyment.

But it is not only from the close association, between the ideas of labour, and painful coercion, that the difficulty in this case proceeds.

Unaccustomed to act upon the motives proper to influence him in his new condition, the negro cannot easily apprehend their nature or their force. When you talk to him of the rewards of industry, and the evil consequences of indolence, you speak a language he can but very imperfectly understand. Hopes and distant fears, as incentives to work, are to him as a new science whereof he has the very elements to learn; or rather like senses, the organs of which are become from want of use inflexible and unsusceptible. You might as reasonably expect a deaf man to march by beat of the drum.

To reclaim an *Indian* from his vagrant habits,
and

and prevail on him to exchange the precarious subsistence of the chace, for the surer returns of the plough, has been found always difficult, and generally impracticable. But the case of the enfranchised negro, though not finally so hopeless, is at first more difficult to remedy. The one is a wild but vigorous youth, who will not easily submit to the drill; the other a ricketty infant, in whom from unnatural restraint the muscles of voluntary motion are contracted. The former may revolt from the yoke of discipline, but the latter must be taught to walk.

In the negro, the self-dependency of a rational being, the close connection between his conduct and his natural, or social welfare, are ideas perfectly new; for in his past state, the ordinary prudential lessons of experience, have been entirely wanting. To speak more properly, they have been inverted. Encrease of labour, has by impairing his health and strength, diminished his bodily comforts without adding to his external enjoyments. His subsistence, has been proportioned to his imbecilities, rather than to his powers of exertion: when able to do least for the master, he has received the most from him; and inaction, when sickness produced a respite from his labours, has been the parent rather of plenty, than of want.

But it would require researches into the human heart, deeper than either my time or my

powers

powers will allow me to pursue, to shew in detail, how greatly the sources of industrious and
virtuous character are ruined by this unnatural
bondage.

Enough has been said to prove, that France
will have abundant difficulty to reconcile with
freedom, the speedy and full restitution of agriculture in her colonies; and she will in consequence
be actuated by strong temptation, to restore if
possible, the coercion of the drivers; while the
same causes will animate in no ordinary degree
the resistance of the negroes. If industry is
odious from the mere remembrance of its acci-
dental connection with their former state; how
much more will they recoil from it with horror,
when the restitution of that state is its avowed
attendant; when the new found and kindly
though yet feeble, motives of reason are to be
withdrawn, and perpetual labour again set before
them in alliance with the compelling cart-whip!

It is not here, that popular spirit, which the
harangues of a demagogue, or the huzzas of a
mob, may be necessary to inflame; it is not even
that indignation which might animate a British
bosom against the invading arms of France; but
a feeling far more powerful still, by which the
Republic will be opposed! Love of country
and love of freedom, never excited opposition so
vigorous or determined, as may be expected in a
cause like this! The event involves interests
more

more awfully important to the opponents than ever before gave violence and durability to the quarrels of mankind.

Supposing then that the counter-revolutionary project of the Chief Consul, will certainly excite in the great body of the negroes a determined *inclination* to resist, let us next proceed to en-quire " what are their *means* of resistance ?"

That a considerable proportion of the adult male negroes of St. Domingo have been trained to arms, is unquestionable, nor is it improbable, that a majority of them are now in some degree inured to a military life; and if these could be generally gained over by France, and employed in the execution of her designs, her immediate temporary success might be easy.

But this, is in a high degree improbable; for hitherto, they have shewn an incurable distrust of all the professions of the Republic, made from time to time by her commissioners or other dele-gates, even while her sincerity in promising to maintain their liberty, could not be reasonably doubted.

No considerable bodies of black troops have ever been prevailed upon to join her standard, or seriously attempt to support her government. Negro leaders alone have been able to inspire
them

them with confidence, and though these have often disputed in the field with each other for ascendancy, the governors appointed by France have not been able either by policy, or by force, to make head any where against either party; but have at best been content to obtain from the courtesy of Toussaint a mere shadow of authority, till the Republic, prior to his late constitution, was obliged to make a virtue of necessity, and recognize him as her legitimate general.

It does not seem probable therefore that Buonaparte with all his policy, will be able to obtain the general and steady co-operation of the negro chieftains and their troops; especially if his plan of interior government be of the nature here supposed.

Let it be considered that these men have wives, children, and other dear connections, whose freedom must be guaranteed with their own, as a necessary basis of any agreement to which they could be expected to subscribe; and if a moderate estimate of the number of these relatives, be added to the probable number of the men accustomed to bear arms, and the sum of both deducted from the population of the island, the residue could scarcely be very great. It would certainly be too small to answer the views here ascribed to the planters and to the Consul,

or

or to admit of the secure re-establishment of the old system in St. Domingo.

Of that system, complexional distinction is too well known, to be a necessary cement, and were even a fourth part only of the negroes to be left in the same condition with the white inhabitants, while the latter had almost exclusively the property of the land and slaves, their safety would probably soon be found to demand a general emancipation.

Were a majority of these black soldiers to cooperate with France, it would soon be fatal as I am about to shew, to the British Islands. But for the present, in order to take the most probable view of the prospects before us, I will assume what seems far the most likely event, that the Consul will not be able to conciliate for the purpose supposed, any large part of these very formidable opponents.

The contest then is to be, as Buonaparte seems by the magnitude of his armaments to expect, not between armies of negroes opposed to each other, but between those natives of the torrid zone, and European troops. Let us enquire on which side, when such are the combatants, lies the probability of success.

That European soldiers have to experience peculiar difficulties in West India warfare in general, is well known. It may be useful however

ever to take a a distinct view of these difficulties, before I point out their fearful aggravation, in a war against the new description of enemies to which the French troops will be opposed.

That disease is infinitely more fatal to Europeans in that climate, than the sword of the most formidable adversary, the British Expeditions to the West Indies in all modern wars, but especially in the last, have fully and painfully evinced. The causes however are but superficially known and considered in this country.

Among all the facts adduced by the West India party in justification of the African trade, the least disputable perhaps is this, that laborious exercise and exposure to the sun in a tropical climate, are destructive to European constitutions. Hence in all the departments of civil life in the West Indies, vigorous labour, especially in the open air, is allotted almost exclusively to the negroes; the very lowest of the whites being only the surveyors of their labours, without any participation in the muscular toil.

Yet even of the white overseers, men generally either natives of the climate, or of the lower order of emigrants from Europe, and consequently of the hardiest habits of body, a great proportion is cut off in the prime of life, by the diseases of the climate.

Exposure to the sun is alone sufficient to produce this effect without the aid of bodily labour, and

to

to produce it on persons who like these overseers, have the advantages of dry and airy lodgings, and wholesome food, and the same comforts in sickness with the most opulent of their employers. How much more fatally then must the same causes operate upon men, who besides exposure to the elements, are obliged to undergo all the fatigues of military service, who are often obliged to act as centinels in the open air obnoxious to the pernicious dews of the climate during the midnight hours, who when encamped in the open country find their tents but a miserable shelter from the tropical rains, and in time of sickness are crowded together in an hospital, mutually incommoding and infecting each other, and without any but that wholesale attention, which gives a cheerless and ineffectual aid to feeble and sinking nature!

Thus circumstanced, it is not strange that the baneful properties of the climate are felt by the poor soldier with a peculiar degre of malignity; and it is to these ordinary causes, more than to that dreaded name the *yellow fever*, that our deplorable losses by sickness in our West India armies are imputable: though other circumstances equally inseparable from a military life, as well as the peculiar difficulty of supplying an army in a West India Island with many articles essential to the health of Europeans

in

in a hot climate, might be pointed out as concurrent sources of disease and mortality.

Of all these disadvantages, the difference of
seasons, the less or greater degree of attention
used by Commanders in Chief, and other adventitious circumstances, may no doubt aggravate
or diminish the mischief; but disease and death
ever have been, and ever will be found, march-
ing in the train of a West India army, and cutting down its battalions with great and deplorable rapidity.

With these most formidable evils affecting
the troops themselves, many others of different
kinds concur to stop the march of conquest between the tropics, and to shorten its reign.

The enormous expence of transporting recruits from Europe, the costly and wasteful
conveyance of military stores and provisions,
and the perishable nature of most of them in a
tropical climate, the frequent losses by sea risk
and still more, the impossibility of effectually checking abuses in that distant field, and
the heavy expence fairly attending every service performed in it, are great and obvious disadvantages of West India warfare: their magnitude and ruinous nature this country has too
fully experienced.

To place a short-lived army in those Islands
costs more perhaps than would suffice for an ordinary campaign; and its services afterwards

are

are far more chargeable, than the same operations would be in any other part of the world.

Nothing could have made such wasteful war endurable by this nation, but the brilliancy and brevity which have generally attended our West India expeditions. I speak not of the fatal enterprise too long persevered in against St. Domingo; a measure which certainly was persisted in and endured with a patience truly astonishing; but let it be remembered that the awful questions at issue in the late war, gave to every undertaking by which the general event might be influenced, a gigantic importance; and seemed to justify sacrifices, to which the worth of the immediate object bore no proportion.

In every other case, and in all former wars, the briefness of active hostilities by European arms, whether French or English, in the West Indies, has greatly palliated the evils that always attend them in that field. A few thousands of white troops on each side, when masters of the sea, or able to elude a superior fleet, alternately surprised a hostile Island, or reduced a fortress; and the operations were commonly so short, that the enterprise and event were usually announced in the same Gazette.

During all such hostilities, the negroes on both sides were held in a strict neutrality: the quarrel between the nations was not worth the peril

of

of employing such allies : the contest therefore lay only between the European garrisons or militia, and the small armies employed in invasion : the scale of war was as minute, as its operations were transitory.

How widely different will be the circumstances of the approaching contest, if a contest be really at hand, between France and negro freedom in the West Indies!!!

To speak of St. Domingo alone; an Island containing at least 45,000 square miles* and half a million perhaps of people, is to be subdued! The time usually spent in West India conquest would not suffice for an unobstructed march across its openest territory. It abounds in natural fastnesses, in passes formidable to an invader, in woods hardly penetrable, in mountains which the panting European would find inaccessible, even if disencumbered of his arms. Here then war is not likely to be soon at the end of its journey.— Its operations must be multiform, extensive, laborious, and long protracted.

If to reduce the whole interior country to effectual submission, will be a tedious as well as

* Geographers differ greatly as to the extent of St. Domingo : Guthrie describes it to be 450 miles long and 150 broad; Mr. Edwards in his history of that Island, page 122, makes it only 390 in length, and 140 in breadth.—I have followed the latter estimate, but with a large deduction for the great irregularity in the breadth.

an arduous work, to fix its subjection permanently must be far more so : to the incalculable
difficulties and hardships of war between the tropics, must be added its European extent and
perseverance.

But when we consider the *new enemy* to be
encountered, these obstacles, great and unprecedented though they are in themselves, swell
into a far greater and less superable magnitude.

To the sickly troops of the invading army,
would be opposed men entirely exempt from the
debilitating influence of the climate, men to
whom the yellow fever is unknown, who are
accustomed to endure the severest labour under a
vertical sun, and who neither sicken from the
excessive heat, nor the occasional humidity, of
the atmosphere.

While the French soldier would sink with fatigue, and contract perhaps a mortal disease, by
an ordinary European march, the negro rather
exhiliarated, than oppressed, by the solar blaze
that exhausts his opponent, at least equally ro-
bust with him, and far more agile by constitution and habits, would advance or retreat the
same distance as matter rather of recreation
than toil, and with a rapidity of which the other
is in that climate quite incapable.

While the white soldier must be maintained
by imported provisions, which cannot without
great difficulty and expence be conveyed to
him

him far from the sea coast, the latter, would find in the most interior parts of the Island, and even on the tops of the mountains, enough of vege‧table food to support his hardy nature, and hold it independently of all the chances of war. The soil itself is his inexhaustible magazine; rapidly producing for him by the briefest and easiest culture, and even by its own spontaneous gift, the esculent plants, and fruits, on which he well knows how to subsist, especially now that the fertile cane lands have for the most part been given up to the culture of provisions.

Accustomed to live on a mere pittance, and to endure nakedness as well as hunger, it is scarcely possible to reduce him by cutting off his supplies; he may therefore leave disease and waste to fight his battles, and find in retreat and delay, certain expeditens to frustrate the most powerful invasion.

The very surface of the country presents infallible means of harassing and destroying an invading army by a desultory system of war.

By the impetuous torrents that rush in the rainy season from the mountains to the sea, every West India Island is broken into innumerable deep ravines, or as they are called in the English-creole dialect "*guts*," so that in general it is impossible to proceed a mile without meeting one of these guts or ravines. Their sides are often too steep to be descended with ease, and

F   are

are besides usually covered with trees and
bushes; the high roads are therefore continued
across these difficult passes by embankments or
bridges above or below; which it is impossible
for a horseman, and even difficult sometimes
for a foot passenger unused to the country, to
cross.

It is obvious how this circumstance might be
improved, not merely for the purposes of ambus-
cade, but, by the easy expedient of breaking
down the bridges and embankments, to stop the
advance of an enemy : indeed it is far more difficult to preserve these roads, than to destroy
them; as they are frequently broken up by the
torrents in the rainy season, and not repaired
without considerable labour and expence.

Even where such difficulties as these do not
present themselves, as in the more level parts of
the Islands, or where the mountains do not rise
very abruptly, there are still obstacles of a very
formidable nature to the advances of an invading army. In the uncultivated part of the country, the underwood is so dense and thorny as not
to be easily penetrated, except by the negroes,
whose dexterity in passing through the woods
by the help of their cutlasses or hatchets is ad-
mirable; and even in the cultivated ground,
from the high growth of the canes, coffee, and
most other tropical productions, an army could
not advance out of the beaten roads, without
clearing

clearing their way by pioneers almost at every footstep, and being continually exposed to ambuscades.

To employ cavalry in such a country is obviously a hopeless expedient ; as for the reasons assigned, the roads might easily be destroyed so as to make the passage of a troop of horse impracticable. Their restitution by the hands of white men would be no easy task; and in some places perhaps the labour of an army for a day would not repair a breach that might be made in a single hour. Besides that in passing these roads the troops would be continually liable to be flanked by ambuscades, they would by being mounted present fairer marks to a lurking enemy, whom when discovered and routed they could not pursue with effect. The fate of a party of the St. Vincent's volunteers who went out on horseback to attack the Charribbs in the late war, sufficiently illustrates this remark.

The places of retreat for the negroes when defeated would of course be the woods and mountains; where it would not only be impossible for horse, but even extremely difficult for European infantry to follow.

The superiority of the negro in that climate is in no point more remarkable than in the dispatch and facility with which he ascends and descends the steepest sides of the mountains, without

without falling or losing his breath; a faculty
which, no doubt, he chiefly owes to long and
early habit in the cultivation of those high and
steep acclivities in which the sugar Islands
abound. By the same habit, greatly assisted by
his not having been accustomed to the restraint
of shoes, and the consequent flexibility of the
muscles of his toes and feet, he is not incom-
moded with the slippery surface of the moun-
tain ridges, though washed with almost continual rains; and where a white man would find it
very difficult to walk steadily, the negro to the
surprise of strangers is seen descending with a
quick step, with a bundle of grass or wood on
his head, without once losing his footsteps, or
dropping his load.

It is on the mountains, that the runaway negroes who abound in the English Islands elude
the pursuit of their masters: it was on the
mountains, that by making a wise but obvious
use of the advantages which I have mentioned,
the Maroon Negroes of Jamaica established
and long maintained their independence; and it
was principally the inaccessibility of such re-
treats, that so long baffled our efforts to conquer
a handful of Charribbs in St. Vincent's.

It would be idle to insist much on the general
advantages of such a native source of defence,
for how many instances are to be met with even
in the history of Europe, of a rude and undis-
ciplined

ciplined people destitute of all other warlike resources, presenting successfully the banier of a mountainous country, to long continued efforts made by powerful nations to subdue them?

But for the reasons already assigned this barrier is far more formidable between the tropics than in the temperate climate of Europe; nor had the Welch, Swiss, or Corsican mountaineers, the same constitutional superiority over their invaders, that the negroes of the sugar Islands possess in their own mountains over the European soldier. *

When on the whole I consider merely the physical disparity between these hardy children of the sun in their native climate, and troops from the temperate zone, I could almost compare the supposed contest, to a battle in the water between a seaman and a shark, or in the air between an æronaut and an eagle.

Does any man doubt whether these new soldiers have courage to second their natural advantages; let him enquire into the military

---

* So strongly were these considerations felt by our gallant Officers who had to conflict on a very small scale with this new enemy in the Windward Islands during the insurrections, and on the re-capture of St. Lucia, that they were obliged to employ negroes for many of the more laborious services ; and called the corps they were composed of, emphatically enough, *" fa-*
" tigue parties."

cha-

character of the black corps which Great Britain herself has raised in the late war, as well as of those by whom her brave armies have been successfully resisted. Let him advert for instance to the following passage in the letter of Lieut. Gen. Trigge that announced the capture of St. Martin's:—"*I have peculiar satis-* "*faction in being able to add that the eighth* "*West India regiment, formed within the three* "*last years and composed almost entirely of* "NEW NEGROES, *who never before had seen an* "*enemy, engaged with a degree of gallantry,* "*and behaved in a manner that would do honor* "*to any troops.*" (London Gazette, May 11th, 1801). These men fought in a cause which however good was certainly not to them so animating as the defence of their private freedom.

I have hitherto considered the difficulty that will attend the supposed enterprise while a standard of resistance is maintained. But the restitution of the old system of slavery will require much more than conquest and general submission. It is not enough to subdue the resisting negroes ; they must be permanently kept in subjection, and in active obedience to their private masters. They must not only be compelled to throw down the musket, but to resume the hoe, and to submit again quietly to the whip!

To govern by military power men who are not

not soldiers, is for the ordinary purposes of civil
government, a plain and easy expedient, and in
a polished state of society the coarse engine
when once put into action possesses, for a time
at least, irresistible force. But its impulse is rather of a benumbing, than a stimulating kind.
The terror it inspires will make men tame, and
passive, but it is ill fitted to enforce the equable
and persevering performance of active duties.
The dread of military execution may disperse a
mob, or enforce the prompt payment of a sub-
sidy; but to oblige men to be industrious and
orderly in the walks of private life, we must resort to sanctions less severe, and more capable
of frequent application.

The notion of agricultural labour being enforced by the continual presence of soldiers in
the field, is too evidently absurd to demand
serious consideration. We need not resort to
the peculiarities of the climate to shew the utter
impracticability of such a mode of coercion; and
as to punishment for past idleness (of which we
have shewn the inefficacy in the case of men
brutalized by having been *driven;*) what pains
could military power hold out as ordinary means
of discipline, more formidable than the cart
whip! The sentence of a Court Martial could
not be more prompt or more decisive than the
mandate of the Overseer.

To maintain however large armies permanently

nently on the spot, though probably ineffectual,
as well as grievously exhausting to the state,
would be undeniably necessary; for it would be
preposterous to suppose that negroes once free,
and bent again by force of arms to the yoke,
could be kept in subjection by means less vigorous. The case of Ireland, where for purposes
far different indeed, means in some degree similar
have been necessarily employed, may in this respect faintly illustrate that of St. Domingo.

Independently of all other considerations, the
great bond of submission upon the minds of the
negroes, is if I mistake not, dissolved for ever.

A strange but fortunate prejudice, the crea-
ture of early terror, fostered by ignorance and
habit, secured in great measure the tranquillity
of these colonies before their revolutions; and
forms the great security of all the Islands wherein slavery still prevails. I mean that *nameless
and undefined idea of terror, connected in the
mind of a negro slave, with the notion of resistance to a white man and a master.*

It is not by comparing the temptations to dis-
obey, with the pain of the worst punishment to
be inflicted for disobedience, that the slave is
kept in submission, or prevented even from raising his hand against his lord. The whip indeed urges him to labour, and the fear of it may
overcome the lassitude, or indolence of nature;
but that which makes him submit to such discipline,

pline, subdue his naturally impetuous and vindictive feelings, be implicit in his active obedience,
at least while under the eye of a master, and
submit to privations and restraints innumerable
without a murmur; in short, that which supports
the master's authority, and ensures his safety, is a
strong and indefinite terror, which the slave from
his earliest years, or from the period of his importation from Africa, has attached to the idea of
active resistance; and which has been strengthened daily more and more, by habit, and the
universal example of his fellow slaves.

Like other phantoms of the imagination (as
for instance the fear of spirits) it is not to be
corrected by reason; and like our sense of the
sublime, it operates even with greater force from
its obscure and indefinite nature.

Without the solution which this principle af-
fords,, the passive submission of the West India
negroes to a very small and often unarmed minority of white men, and the extreme rarity of any
act of individual vengeance on a master, would be
wholly inexplicable; for in most of the Islands
the law has annexed no more dreadful mode of
execution than hanging, either to rebellion or
to murder; yet insurrections, especially in the
old islands, are very rare; and the murder of a
master by his slave, a crime scarcely ever heard
of, except in a general revolt.

These facts cannot proceed from the absence of
resentful

resentful feelings; for towards persons of their own colour, negroes are uncommonly violent and vindictive; and murder is among them no unusual crime. Nay, it has sometimes happened, that resentment of some great wrong received from a master, instead of leading to violences against him personally, has induced them to indulge the desire of vengeance at the expence of their own destruction, in order to deprive him of his property. Within a few years, and in a single island, three instances occurred of slaves putting themselves to death, avowedly from this motive; and in one case, the man while in great torments from the fractures and dislocations caused by jumping down a deep well, gloried in what he had done; telling his master with exultation, " *that he had lost his most valuable slave.*"

It is obvious that such revenge and desperation must often be fatal to the master, if some principle stronger than the fear of death itself were not his protection.

It would be tedious to mention all the facts and considerations from which the existence of such a principle may be farther demonstrated; but no man of reflexion can have resided long in the West Indies without perceiving it, and relying on it more than on the laws or the government, for his security.

This principle of action, like most others, that have their origin, not in reason, but in ignorance

norance and habit, *when once subverted can never be renewed.* The negro, who has been ele-
vated to the same social freedom with his former
master, and has drawn aside the veil by which
the weak pedestal of former authority was con-
cealed, can no more regard the one with a superstitious reverence, nor yield a blind obedience to
the other. The spell is finally dissolved.

More especially must this prejudice be incapable of renewal, when the practical lesson has
been, not only that white men and masters may
be resisted, but even confronted in arms, without those nameless dreadful consequences at
which the soul was formerly appalled.

It will be no less impossible again to breathe
into such men the terrors which kept them in
subjection, than it would be to renew in a philo-
sopher the superstitions of the nursery, so that he
should again believe in giants and magicians; or
to frighten a man of mature age with the rod of
his schoolmaster. If bowed anew under the former system, they will submit perhaps, while reason shews them the impracticability of resistance, but no longer; and it is not this prudential
thinking, obedience, that will enable the white
Colonists to maintain their authority, with their
former small proportion of numbers, and scanty
means of military defence.

I consider this change in the *ideas,* of the negroes as the most invincible of bars to the permanent

manent restitution of the slave system in the French Islands: but the revolution that has taken place in their *habits*, is a concurrent and very formidable obstacle. The weight of the chain so long thrown off would now be felt with an increased and intolerable pressure; and a restless desire to escape from it, would probably be superior to the apprehension of the most real and imminent dangers of resistance.

Insurrection therefore would long continue to find frequent and bloody employment for the large garrisons of Guadaloupe and St. Domingo; till the Mother Country, wearied with the expence of life and treasure in recruiting them, would relax in her efforts, and successful rebellion give a new birth to negro freedom.

I am, &c. &c.

LETTER III.

[77]

LETTER III.

Sir,

I HAVE thus far endea-
voured to illustrate the true nature of the contest in which France has probably embarked; and
have laid before you some considerations from
which the best conjecture may be formed of the
immediate event; especially in relation to that
great Island, which may perhaps be destined to
be the cradle of the liberty, of the African race,
as it formerly was of their bondage, in the Western world.

To prove that the restitution of the yoke they
have broken will not be easily effected, was a
necessary preliminary to that which is more immediately the subject of our present enquiry, the
determining *what consequences interesting to
Great Britain this great enterprise is likely to
produce.*

But

But that branch of our subject appeared to me to have a further, and substantive, importance. The policy of this country since the preliminaries of Peace were signed, seems to have been greatly affected by an opinion that a counter-revolution in the French Colonies, was an object not only desired by the Republic, and salutary to our own West India Islands, but a highly practicable work; and I know not to what dangerous lengths the same groundless expectation may continue to prevail and to influence our public counsels*.

I proceed to consider first the probable effects of a failure in this undertaking; and shall next enquire, what consequences are likely to flow from the opposite, and more unlikely event, that of its success.

In contemplating the former case, the public opinion seems so far to have anticipated my con-

* It seems probable that but for such an expectation France would not have been permitted to send such vast armaments to the West Indies before a Peace was definitively sealed. On the prudence of such a permission I presume not to offer an opinion, as the grounds of it are not yet before the public. Much confidence is due to the prudence of administration, and it is presumable that this courtesy to the Republic was founded upon considerations that could not with propriety be disclosed. As the case now stands before the public, the dissatisfaction and anxiety on this subject, expressed by a learned and very intelligent Member of the House of Commons, seem by no means ill founded.

clusions,

clusions, as to regard the establishment of a negro state, or even a community of free negroes under the government of France, in the West Indies, as likely to prove fatal in its consequences to our sugar Colonies.

The danger of such a political phenomenon in point of precedent, on which great stress has been laid, is sufficiently obvious. But that danger is not in my apprehension the greatest ground of alarm: for there is a state of extreme degradation in which man is little affected by political argument, even in the persuasive form of example; and a jacobin would probably find the field-negro of Jamaica, a pupil less susceptible than even the Copht of Grand Cairo.

But in the event here first supposed, Propagandists would soon be found, with physical force enough to break the chains of their sable brethren, and with arms to put into their hands; or at least with power to usurp the territory to which they belong, and give them masters of a new complexion.

The natural and ordinary appetite in the founders of an infant state, for enlargement of dominion, would be whetted by the richness of the neighbouring spoil, by the facility of conquest, and by a pretext which would give to usurpation the appearance of generosity and justice. If the little Grecian republics, thought it an honourable cause of war, to deliver men of
the

the same extraction, from the domination of those
whom they called tyrants; how much more spe-
ciously might the hostilities of the negro chiefs
of St. Domingo be justified, by the degrading
bondage of their African brethren ! Nor would
policy fail to co-operate very powerfully with
these motives. The security of their own freedom
would hardly be compatible with the continuance of negro slavery in all the surrounding
Islands; and they would see in the bondage of
Cuba and Jamaica, a yoke that would probably
be refitted to their own necks, if the powers of
Europe should ever be able to replace it. While
a skin, of the same tincture with their own,
should every where else in the West Indies, and
even in the skirts of the same visible horizon,
be a badge of perpetual slavery, how could
they possibly regard their white neighbours
with confidence; or feel that they held their
own new social character and privileges by a safe
and peaceable tenure?

The neutrality of Toussaint, from the time
of the evacuation of St. Domingo by our troops
to the end of the war, is no argument for the
expectation of the same policy in future. It
was the result of a compact made by him, in
very critical and arduous circumstances : so at
least we are warranted by strong appearances, as
well as general and uncontradicted report, to believe; and that extraordinary man is said to be
distin-

distinguished by inviolable fidelity to his engagements.

But if he, and the people of St. Domingo in general, were weak enough to believe Great Britain, sincerely disposed to favour the cause of negro freedom in the West Indies, they must be already convinced of their mistake. They have seen the bar of our naval hostilities removed from the coasts and the harbours of France in order that naval armaments might proceed against them; before notice of the Peace, should put them on their guard; and this not only while they were observing a strict neutrality towards us, but while our quarrel with the Republic was not yet definitively ended. They will know that the British Cabinet chose even to encounter some national anxiety rather than not acquiesce in a measure hostile to the negroes of St. Domingo.

If still undeceived, it is probable they will not long remain so, unless you, Sir, and your colleagues should cease to behold with that complacency which has been hitherto manifested, this project of the Court of the Thuilleries.

Situated as Jamaica is, it is scarcely possible, that in the approaching contest, we should observe an exact neutrality of conduct in that Colony unless very rigid prohibitions, such as will not readily flow from the disposition which seems at this juncture to prevail, are speedily issued and

G   enforced.

enforced. The ships of France will perhaps be
refitted in the harbours of that island, or at least
kindly received there; and from thence as convenient magazines, the fleet and army of St.
Domingo, will probably draw many essential
supplies. Shall we treat the resisting negroes
with equal favor? I presume, Sir, you are not
prepared to risque another war with France by
acting on this occasion the part she took with
our own revolted colonies; and if you were, I am
sure that the people of Jamaica would not well
second your intentions; you will find it difficult
even during this *bellum servile*, to restrain them
by the strongest interdictions from active co-
operation with the assailants.

To a determined spirit of hostility against our
Islands, the negroes should they triumph in the
approaching contest will add new energies of
character, and new means of annoyance. It is
by a struggle for political independence, or social freedom, that the warlike faculties of a
people are most powerfully called forth, and the
military spirit created. But for independency,
the negroes of St. Domingo cannot properly be
said yet to have fought; much less for that far
more interesting stake " private freedom," as
opposed to West India bondage.

They broke the yoke indeed by insurrection,
and some barbarous conflicts ensued; but the
resistance

resistance of the masters was short, as well as feeble; and the struggle was no more fitted to form them into soldiers, than the massacres of Paris were to discipline its ferocious insurgents.

The resistance afterwards made to the British arms, furnished no doubt a better school; but the cause was hardly understood to be that of freedom, as opposed to domestic slavery. To restore the whips and the drivers, was not, in profession at least, the object of our invasion, and to reduce the interior of the Island, was hardly a part of our attempt. We seized on many of their ports, and their fortresses, on the coast; but to the negroes of the interior the question might seem to be little more than whether the pennants of France or Great Britain should fly in their harbours; and in that question they, who naturally regarded all Europeans as enemies, and the French in general as exasperated foes, probably felt little interest beyond what their leaders cloathed with some shew of French authority, and wishing to conciliate the Republic, laboured to inspire. Considerable bodies of ill-armed troops were drawn together, and hemmed in our garrisons, within the walls of the fortifications which they occupied, or within such a narrow border of surrounding territory, as European soldiers could traverse by a single march in that climate: but it was as impossible for the negroes, destitute as
they

they were of artillery and of most other means of
regular warfare, to attack us in our fortified
posts, as for our sickly and much divided forces,
to march under a vertical sun, through that
extensive country, in quest of an enemy in the
open field.   Regular battles therefore were unknown and even skirmishes not very frequent.—
From the time of our reducing the important
places on the coast, to the final evacuation of
them, the war resembled a long blockade: the
invaders and invaded were for the most part
alike inactive, and disease was the only, but the
effectual assailant, to which British courage and
perseverance, were at length obliged to submit.

That by these contests, and the subsequent
civil broils, soldiers have been formed in sufficient
abundance to make the black colonists dangerous
neighbours is not very doubtful: but if I judge
rightly of the approaching struggle, military
skill and military habits will rise among them
to a much higher pitch, and will be aided by
a proud sense, not of equality merely, but of superiority, in war, to the troops of Europe.

Not only a spirit of conquest, the ordinary
growth of this character, may be expected to
follow; but employment for the black legions
will become necessary to internal repose.—For
man, military man at least, is nearly the same
character between the tropics as in the temperate
zone;

zone; and St. Domingo like ancient Rome, or modern France, will have become a military Republic.

It is needless to insist further on the dangerous consequences to be apprehended from the supposed triumph of the arms of the negroes, as they are on all hands perceived and acknowledged. But between the entire success of the plans of France, and the total subversion of her authority and influence, there is a middle issue, to the probability and the tendency of which the public seems not to have sufficiently adverted : I mean that of a compromise, by which the sovereignty of the Republic may be acknowledged, and negro liberty at the same time maintained.

There is a point beyond which ineffectual efforts to restore the former system, will probably not be extended ; and from the nature of the impending contest this crisis is probably not very remote. It may be accelerated, by a new revolution not unlikely to happen in the government of the Republic; and by the natural disposition in the authors of a revolution to reverse the measures of their predecessors in authority.

Now, whenever that period comes, it can hardly be supposed that France in sheathing the sword, will needlessly renounce the sceptre. Unable to restore the planters, she will at least

attempt

attempt to restore the political supremacy of the
Republic; and if the negroes cannot again be
made slaves, she will invite them to enjoy their
freedom under the protection of the tri-coloured
flag. Like Great Britain, in the case of the
North American Colonies, she will attempt conciliation, when force is found inefficacious, and
probably with better success; for a separation
from the mother country in Europe, however desirable it may have been thought for the self-
dependent, and commercial colonies, of the
Northern Continent, can never be the interest
of a West India Island.

France, in a word, will in the supposed event
be glad to preserve the sovereignty of the Island
upon terms to which the negroes will readily
subscribe: they will continue free, but will ac-
knowledge themselves French citizens or subjects.

Or let it here be supposed, that my notions of
the present design of the Chief Consul are un-
founded; and that these great armaments have
been dispatched, not to alter the condition of
the negroes, but merely to overturn the Constitution and Government of Toussaint; and let
it also be supposed that this comparatively easy
enterprise will be crowned with immediate success; and what will be the obvious immediate
consequence? In this case, as well as in the
former,

former, we have our natural enemy, the gigantic rival of our greatness, placed in a capacity of annoyance, not less formidable, than unparalleled.

Behold in this single Island a population, of at least two hundred thousand adult male negroes* of whom probably, a third part are already inured in some degree to arms, at the door of our most valuable settlement, and ready to assist the ambition of the Republic for any purpose not adverse to their freedom, but most of all for that of conquering the slave-peopled islands of Great Britain!

* This to European ideas may appear too large a proportion of men, if the whole population does not exceed half a million; but let it be observed, that there is always a vast disproportion of numbers between the sexes among the colonial negroes, the males being by far the more numerous, and that the rising generation is unhappily very thin compared to the parent stocks. Both these known circumstances of West India population are most prominent where the recent importations from Africa have been greatest; and these were unusually great in St. Domingo within a few years immediately preceding the revolution. In a general account of the state of the West Indies published in 1778 there is an account of the population of the French part of this Island wherein the slaves are stated to amount to 250,000 only, though the author evidently wishes to give strong ideas of the importance of the Colony; yet by official returns in 1790 which have been already noticed, they amounted to 480,000 and Mr. B. Edwards gives that as the true number about the same period. Hist. of St. Domingo, page 10.

Hitherto,

Hitherto, the West India Colonies, have furnished few or no resources of offensive war to their European masters. They have in their strongest state, demanded protection, rather than ministered assistance. Endangered within by a source of perpetual insecurity, by a system which precluded the hope of voluntary fidelity in the great mass of the inhabitants, all that the free Colonists could be expected to do for the parent state in war, and more than they have always effected, has been to guard themselves by militia establishments, from insurrections of their slaves; and to second, in some small measure, the efforts of their European defenders, in repelling invasion.

Many an effective regiment has been reduced to a mere name in their hospitals; but not one regular corps, till the alarming exigencies of the late war, led to the before untried expedient of enrolling a regiment or two of negroes, was ever raised in the West Indies. Instead therefore of strengthening the belligerent arm of the parent state, they drained away its vigour; armies powerful at the opening of a campaign, have been divided and broken down to recruit their garrisons, or to suppress their revolted slaves.

With such imbecilities and disadvantages, which Great Britain must still continue to sustain in her colonies, let us for a moment contrast

trast the new situation of France on the supposed pacification with the negroes.

She will stand in need of no armies from Europe. The diversion of force in this quarter,
the enormous expence, the danger of the passage, with the dreadful mortality, to which European troops are subject in a West India campaign, may all be saved. St. Domingo alone,
will furnish disposable troops enough, to out-
number the utmost collective force which we
can possibly spare for the defence of all our
islands; of troops, to whom the peculiarities of
the climate are salubrious, instead of destructive;
and marches under a vertical sun neither exhausting nor laborious.

Nor will her future hostilities be subject to
any diversion by the defence of those Colonies
of her own in which liberty shall remain. Their
internal strength will bid defiance to invasion, as
in the late war we have too fully experienced.
What is still more formidable, the attractions of
her new system, and the very complexion of her
troops, will ensure to her in every slave Colony
she invades, numerous and irresistible allies, ready
not only to facilitate, but to perpetuate her conquests.

I challenge any man, acquainted with the
West Indies, or with the history of warfare in
that country, to point out any possible means by
which

which our islands, and especially Jamaica, could be effectually defended against such fearful odds as these!

Of the inclination of France when opportunity may invite, to strip us of our sugar Colonies, little doubt can be entertained; but in the case supposed new motives would arise to strengthen the ordinary impulses of commercial rivalship and ambition.

We suppose her baffled in the attempt to restore the agricultural wealth of St. Domingo, and obliged to acquiesce in its remaining for a long time barren of almost all but military advantages. Without the produce of this great and fertile Island under industrious culture, competition with Great Britain in the sugar markets of Europe will be impossible; and the consumption of France herself, must in a considerable degree be supplied by the British Planter. Is it likely then, that she will suffer us to retain such an ascendancy, and such golden advantages, at her expence, when the means of wresting them from us will be at once easy and obvious? No! From the moment that St. Domingo is found incapable of being speedily restored to its former value, the rich Island of Jamaica, will become an object of jealousy and envy that France will not have justice or moderation enough to resist; and will be thought

perhaps

perhaps a reasonable indemnity for the ir-
reclaimable state of her own Colonies, produced in some measure as it may seem to have
been, by the maritime hostilities of this country.

" She cut us off from our Colonies" might the
French Politician say of Great Britain " while
" our influence or our arms might have remedied
" the recent effects of insurrection ; she ceased
" to do so, only when those effects were incur-
" able ; it is just that she should furnish an in-
" demnity. Instead of a colony of labourers,
" she has allowed us to regain only a colony
" of soldiers. We have found the plough-share
" beat into a sword ; and must make the only
" remaining use of our dominion, by employing
" that sword against her. Since the negroes
" will not resume their hoes, let us avail our-
" selves of their muskets. By means of these
" African auxiliaries, we shall wound Carthage
" in the most vulnerable side, clip the wings
" of her commerce, and enrich ourselves with
" her spoils !"

Against the injustice of this language, I fear
the morality of a French statesman would not
very strongly revolt; and to its policy, it seems
not easy to find a very satisfactory objection.
Were there even no expedients to prevent the enfranchisement of the Jamaica slaves from being
an immediate result of the supposed conquest; and
supposing

supposing that no advantages, would, in that case, redound to the French commerce or revenue; still a severe blow would be given to the resources and the power of Great Britain, and to that decided maritime superiority, which is at once the curb and the humiliation of the Republic.

How far reluctance to enter on a new war, would for a while counterpoise these temptations, I leave to the consideration of those who are best qualified to estimate the general probabilities of an abiding pacific disposition in the government of that powerful and impetuous people. But let it be taken into the calculation that the re-establishment of her West India commerce, and the retrieval of her colonial wealth, must have been leading motives with France in the late pacification; and that in proportion therefore as these objects are found unattainable, our security for her pacific views will probably be impaired. We may add, it will be still more diminished by a state of things which may furnish her with new and effectual means of annoying her old enemy in a distant quarter of the world. Instead of the love of general peace, proving a protection to Jamaica, the temptation offered by that Island may be fatal to the general peace.

The defence of our wooden walls, will naturally present itself to an English mind, as a possible safeguard to our Islands; even under circum-

stances

stances the most perilous. Of this dependence in the case supposed, I shall shew the extreme insecurity; but will defer that consideration till we have examined another source of dangers, to which the reasoning to be adduced will be equally applicable.

Hitherto, we have supposed that France will not acomplish the restitution of negro bondage. Let us now suppose on the contrary, that this great counter-revolution will be fully effected.

This is an event, to which the public mind has been industriously directed, as an object perfectly desirable for this country. " The res-" toration of order, industry, and subordination, " the subjugation of the refractory negroes, the " destruction of the revolutionary scourge, the " extinction of anarchy, of the jacobin spirit;" and many other specious descriptions, are employed to pourtray this happy change, which yet has been shewn, to have no distinct and definite meaning in the minds of Europeans in general; but which if meant to imply the speedy restitution of industry by force of arms, must necessarily imply in practice the re-establishment of the former bondage.

From this counter-revolution, we are taught as Englishmen to expect none but happy consequences. " It is to *put an end, to the dangerous situation of our own* Islands !" It is
" an

" an object, that the British Ministry *must se-*
cretly if not openly favour; which if *they do*
not actively promote, they must at least cordi-
ally desire !"

The confidence with which such notions are
asserted, is not greater than the credulity with
which they are recieved; though to a man who
extends his researches an inch below the surface
their rashness and unsoundness, are most evident.

We have seen the formidable difficulties, that
must attend the subjugation of the negroes, if
ever finally subdued; and it has I trust, been
satisfactorily proved to you, that supposing such
an object attained, nothing less than the continual presence of an irresistible military force,
can maintain the restored authority of the master, or prevent the most dreadful insurrections.
Now France like Great Britain, formerly maintained but slender garrisons, in her Islands, in
time of Peace. In general they were indeed
rather stronger than our own; but not more than
sufficient to secure their most important fortresses from sudden assault, and by no means
such as to afford the means of any important exterior enterprise.

Hence the chief security of the two Powers
as to their sugar Colonies, on the breaking out
of war. For the purpose of West India conquest, armies were to be sent from Europe; and
time was consequently given to the opposite
Power

Power if vigilant, to make preparations for defence. By a kind of tacit compact, means of offensive warfare were not provided in that distant quarter, except during actual hostilities; and had a considerable force been sent out by either Power during Peace, the other would have remonstrated, and on failure of immediate satisfaction, would have felt sufficient ground for counter-preparation at least, if not even a justifiable cause of war.

But France now, will have an unanswerable pretext for increasing her West India garrisons to any extent she thinks proper: she will even be under an evident necessity, of maintaining in that quarter at all times, a regular force large enough to be utterly inconsistent with the safety of the British Islands.

You admit her right to send to St. Domingo before the sword is well sheathed, 25 sail of the line, and 25,000 men, because the re-establishment of her colonial government requires it. How then can you deny her an equal right, to maintain for the necessary support of that government when re-established, whatever force the case may fairly seem to require? To call on her to reduce her garrisons, to the old peace establishment at St. Domingo, Guadaloupe, or Cayenne, would be a demand to give up anew her slave system in those colonies, and consign the planters to the horrors of a second revolution.

Admitting

Admitting that she has a right, to maintain there a force hitherto unknown in times of Peace, what limits can you put to its dimensions? Who but the governments of those respective Colonies, or the cabinet with which they correspond, shall judge of their interior situations, and of the degree of latent danger to which they may be exposed from the the embers of the newly-extinguished fire? Are we to appoint secret committees to enquire into the plots of the French slaves? If not, by what means shall we determine, how many thousand troops are necessary at Guadaloupe, and how many tens of thousands at St. Domingo, for the purposes of internal security?

If a French Minister wanted an argument to enhance those necessities, he might remind us of the Maroons of Jamaica, or the Charribbs of St. Vincent; and ask us to count our losses by those petty enemies, whose expulsion only could make us safe, before we prescribe limits to her, in the means of overawing and coercing half a million of negroes! It is needless to suppose however, in the Republic, any wish to exceed in her establishments the real exigencies of the case. Without any insidious use of her new situation in the Antilles, it will oblige her to become formidable there to every neighbouring Power. Without any hostile views,

views, she must prepare the means of irresistible future hostility.

I pretend not to determine, to what extent her permanent military establishment must necessarily be enhanced: it is sufficient to say, that beyond the defence of the old fortifications, endangered perpetually by a new internal enemy, she must establish and maintain a military organization in the interior, ramified enough, and strong enough, to overawe the slaves, and to give security and confidence to the masters. Without this, the counter-revolution we are supposing would be fruitless of every thing but blood; and with a permanent force like this, at her command, no hostile neighbour could be safe for a moment. Draughts that would hardly be missed from such an establishment, would be adequate to overpower the strongest garrison we ever maintained during Peace, in the largest of our Islands.

But a more alarming consideration still, arises from the nature of the force of which these new and formidable establishments will certainly in a great degree be composed. That the full success we are now supposing to have crowned the plans of the French Government, can possibly be attained, without a coalition with the negro chiefs, and the assistance of large bodies of their troops, it would be preposterous to imagine. How then are those important auxiliaries to be

H   disposed

disposed of, when the arduous immediate object shall be accomplished? Will France disband these sable legions? Will she tell them to pile their arms in the cane pieces, and submit their backs again to the drivers? That they would acquiesce in such treatment, is not more improbable, than that the government of the Republic would be rash and weak enough to make the experiment. But France will have learnt to appreciate their value as soldiers too well to wish to reduce their numerous and disciplined battalions. She will see in them, not only the necessary support of interior government, but the irresistible instruments of her ambition, and the potentiality of soon wresting from this country the whole of her West India dominions. Rely upon it then Sir that generals *Toussaint, Christopher,* and *Moses,* will not be cashiered; and that France will in future not only outwing you enormously in her military establishments in the Western World, but that her soldiers will be of that formidable description, whose native superiorities I have feebly attempted to delineate*.

---

* A British officer who was taken prisoner on his passage from Jamaica and carried into St. Domingo, has published a short narrative of his adventures in that island, and he states that he saw Toussaint review near the Cape 60,000 well disciplined negroes. (See Major Rainsford's Narrative.)

Let

Let us now take down the map of the West Indies, and cast our eyes on the different geographical points where these dangerous establishments will be formed.

In the first place, we have Cayenne, a settlement to windward of all our Islands and within a short distance of some of the most valuable. Next, Guadaloupe, a large Island in the very centre of the Charribbean chain, and surrounded by British Colonies, at the distance of a few hour's sail:—Lastly, the great Island of St. Domingo, now wholly belonging to France, from which the shores of Jamaica, can be seen, and can be invaded by a passage before the wind, to be made in a single night. Had France selected three military stations, as places of arms, and of rendezvous, for the future conquest of all our sugar colonies, she could not have chosen better. Her invading Power, will stand on tiptoe at the very threshold of every West India Island we possess, ready to rush in upon the first order for hostilities.

Her military establishments at Cayenne, and Guadaloupe, indeed, will naturally be much less than in the vast Island of St. Domingo; but when compared to the ordinary means of defence, in our small adjacent islands, will be equally irresistible. An effective company of regulars for each Island of the windward and leeward Charibbees is more, than in times of

peace

peace we have usually maintained. Some of the smaller Islands, have often been left in the late Peace, without any European troops at all; and as to the petty militia furnished by a scanty free population of a few hundred families, it was rarely called out, or embodied, except during actual war.

What hope could be founded on means of defence like these, against such an army as even Guadaloupe, would now at a day's notice be able to furnish for invasion? To rivet the chains of near 100,000 negroes, will probably require even there, many thousands of regular troops; of whom, for the brief and important purposes, of a *coup de main* against our Islands a considerable part might be drawn from garrison service.

To keep in subjection the re-inslaved negroes at Cayenne, and guard the large, and now much-extended limits of that colony a force equally great will in all likelihood be employed, as the continental situation, makes insurrection there peculiarly easy, and its suppression extremely difficult.* Grenada, would probably give the first temptation to hostile enterprise, from this quarter; and let the history of her late insurrection witness, how hopeless would be her ordinary means of resistance. Thus, without

* The settlement properly called *Cayenne* is divided only by a small river from the Continent of *Guyana.*

taking

taking into account the force of Martinique, and the other Islands, restored by the peace to France; which will also probably soon be garrisoned by negro troops; we should find in every quarter dangers of the most imminent kind,

I confess to you Sir, that when I contemplate this prospect, I am astonished to hear the success of the French expedition spoken of as an event for which Englishmen are to put up their vows. The planter's property might indeed be as safe in Jamaica under the French flag, as in Demerara under the Dutch; and if the Consul cordially shakes hands with negro slavery, I know not why this prospect should even check the same spirit of speculation that lately poured millions of British capital into the soil and the slave markets of colonies soon to revert to an enemy. But to the general interests of the empire, there is a calamity far more fatal than even the dreaded progress of negro-liberty; and that is, the addition of our West India possessions to the other conquests of France. For the country at large, it would be a less dreadful evil, that our sugar colonies should be impoverished or ruined by revolution, than conquered by foreign arms; and less injurious that they should be usurped by a negro state, than by the government of the great nation.

How then Sir are these great public dangers to be averted?

Are

Are we permanently to garrison all our Islands with troops numerous enough to defend them against these new means of invasion, which will be perpetually in their vicinage? The whole standing army of Great Britain, would probably be too small for the purpose; and the ravages of disease would require its triennial renewal. A land press would be necessary, to recruit those fatal garrisons; for death would reduce our regiments, faster than voluntary enrolment could supply them with new levies.

" But our *Fleets*," it may be said, " our ever victorious *Fleets*, are an adequate security." The most obvious and unanswerable objection to this ground of confidence is, what I shall presently consider, the enormous and ruinous waste, not only of the wealth, but the maritime force, of the country, which such a scheme of permanent defence in that climate would involve. But those who think our widely dispersed sugar colonies could be effectually defended by naval force alone, against dangers threatening so continually, and from so many neighbouring points, as in the case now under consideration, have paid very little attention to the history of West India warfare, or to the general nature of maritime defence.

I believe that were any one of our brave and intelligent sea officers to be asked his opinion on this point, the answer would be, that he would not engage with the strongest British squadron that

that ever cruized between the tropics, permanently to prevent under the circumstances here supposed, the invasion of Jamaica alone. Nor do I speak here with any view to opposition by a hostile fleet large as that lately dispatched from France; but desire the admission only, that there will be in the harbours of St. Domingo, vessels or boats of any kind capable of transporting troops across the calm and narrow channel which divides that Island from Jamaica : For with naval means contemptible like these even, an invading army, might be wafted over by night to its destined point, eluding the vigilance, or by the aid of known winds and currents, mocking the pursuit, of the best conducted squadron.

By detailing geographical circumstances which are sufficiently known, it would be easy to prove the difficulty of defending by a naval force alone the coasts of a West India Island, But this detail would be tedious, and I conceive unnecessary. The fallibility of that species of defence every where, against an enterprising enemy, has in some degree been practically proved by the incidents of the late war, and is pretty generally admitted; but it was demonstrated in cases more directly in point, by the West India conquests of the French under the Marquis de Bouillie in the war preceding the last.

If any one supposes that these Islands can
be

be effectually covered by a superior, or even an unresited, fleet; let him explain the reason why Guadaloupe from its re-conquest by Victor Hugues, to the end of the late war, was such a nuisance as it is well known to have been, to our trade in the Charribbean seas. Near 30 English pennants were at one time flying in the neighbourhood of *that Island*, and avowedly ordered to blockade it: And that the attempt was not long or closely prosecuted, could only have arisen from the early discovery of its impracticability; for no enterprise to be compared to this in importance, demanded or engaged, the services of his Majesty's ships on that station. Our men of war in fact were rarely, if ever out of sight, of the harbours of that hostile colony; and after the glorious capture of La Pique they found no enemy bold enough to engage them :- yet supplies of every kind entered the ports of Guadaloupe, and its privateers continually sallied out, to commit depredations on our commerce, and returned with their prizes in safety. Victor Hugues at the same time sent out from this Island more than one petty armament, against our colonies, and those of our allies. It would be a libel on the gallant British Admirals, who successively commanded on that station, to admit these facts, and at the same time to assert, that naval force alone can be expected effectually to preclude the invasion of Jamaica; an Island the defence

of

of which would be liable to the same general
geographical difficulties, with the blockade of
Guadaloupe, and which has a circuit of accessible coast, vastly more extensive.

Let it be considered however that we shall not
in the case supposed, have only a single Island to
cover or to blockade, as was the case during a
large portion of the late war, when Guadaloupe
was almost the sole naval station of importance
in the hands of the enemy to demand the vigilance of our fleets, in the West India seas; or from
which invasion could be apprehended. Widely
different will be the work of shutting up the
enemy in the ports of all the different and
much dispersed colonies whence his new found
force may menace, including the wide-spread
shores of St. Domingo; or that of guarding by
a naval force all our numerous Islands that will
be continually in danger of invasion. For this
arduous purpose, it would be indispensable that
large squadrons should be maintained at the same
time, on many different stations, from which
they could not soon or easily be united; from
Barbadoes in the 59th, to Jamaica in the 77th,
degree of west longitude.

Have we even, any reasonable ground to presume, that our entire mastery of these seas will
in a future war be wholly undisputed? That our
naval force if collected, will be always superior
in strength, as well as in courage and skill, to any
hostile fleet that can be brought to encounter it,

we

we may indeed safely conclude; but that France will be unable to maintain in any quarter, a fleet sufficient to protect an invading armament against any one of our divided squadrons, is surely too much to be relied upon. Able to choose her point of attack, she will naturally select it where we are weakest; and were the war to lie only between St. Domingo and Jamaica, it might not be too much to affirm that places of descent could be chosen, in the passage to which a covering fleet could not intercept the invaders, without either encountering fearful odds by an irrecoverable dispersion, or leaving other parts of the Island open and defenceless.

If more exact ideas of such nautical difficulties are desired, a reference to the official accounts of the many sea engagements in the West Indies, during the American war, but especially during the active campaigns of 1781, and 1782, may amply supply them.

These observations might perhaps suffice to prove, that our wooden walls would be an inadequate and precarious safeguard, against the dangers now in contemplation.

But the most disheartening circumstance still remains. For in either of the events supposed, these new dangers will be of a permanent, unremitting nature; and consequently will require continual preparation for defence. Whether we shall have to stand on our guard, against an
independent

independent negro state, or against free negroes under the government of France, or against the extraordinary means of offensive war that a counter-revolution would necessarily place in the hands of our old enemy, the peril will be such as to threaten us every moment; and must impend over our colonies, as long as the same sources of belligerent strength, stand opposed to the interior imbecility of our own possessions.

It is not an occasional effort of the Republic in that distant field that we shall have to meet by cotemporary exertion; but perennial dangers, against which our means of defence must be equally permanent, and kept up without intermission. Even during peace, they will scarcely be less necessary than in war; for unless the enemy could be bound to give us six months notice previously to the drawing of his sword, defensive armaments could not cross the Atlantic before our most valuable colonies would be lost.

The question therefore, is not, what security might be obtained, by means of such a fleet or such an army as we might send to that distant quarter for a single campaign, or on the spur of some short emergency; but what reliance can be placed on such garrisons, and such stationary squadrons, as we could afford constantly to maintain there.

Without

Without presuming to calculate the value of Jamaica, and the other sugar colonies, and only assuming that it is something short of the full value of his Majesty's European dominions, including our constitution, our liberties and our national independence; I may infer that we cannot afford to protect these colonies at the expence of *ruining our navy;* and if not, to station permanently there fleets large enough for the purpose in question, would not be an allowable, supposing it might be an effectual expedient. It is reported, Sir, that you have dispatched a naval force to Jamaica, strong enough to cope, if needful, with the united squadrons of France and Spain which preceded it. If such be the fact, I condemn not the precaution: but every British heart must lament its necessity.—One powerful enemy, disease, our brave tars will be sure to be assailed by, in that fatal region; and his ravages will not be the less destructive, because they may have no other foe to encounter. The hope of booty or of glory, the interest of a chace, or the looking out for a hostile sail, will no longer aid their spirits against the gloomy spectacle of sickness and death among their mess-mates, and the enervating influence of the climate.

The exemption of the French marine from the samed estructive evils, would aggravate the national

tional mischief of such a scheme of defence, if we should be driven to it as a permanent system. Without keeping a single ship of the line in the West Indies, perhaps even without a hostile intention, the Republic would have the important advantage of diverting and consuming our naval force, as well in peace as in war.—We should have to feed this Minotaur with our best blood continually.—We should probably be obliged to send out every year to be preyed on by tropical diseases, more seamen as recruits, or more entire new ships-companies to supply the waste of death, than were ever annually consumed before in our most bloody maritime wars, and in all the collective services of our marine.

When the mind contemplates this dreadful sacrifice, every other price to be paid for the future protection of our sugar-colonies seems of little account:—we sufficiently discern how well Africa will be avenged; and how probably those colonies, for the sake of which we have hugged fondly to our bosoms that deformed monster the Slave Trade, after its frightful aspect has been laid bare before the eye of the national conscience, may soon by a righteous Providence be made the sources of our humiliation and ruin.

And yet Sir, to you as the Steward of the National Purse, I ought to add the important remark

remark, that such great and enduring efforts of
defensive preparation would not be less fatal to
our finances, than to the lives of our brave soldiers and seamen.—Did the Islands grow not
only sugar but gold, they might be bought too
dear; and the people of this country might
grudge to give for the defence of those colonies
another tenth of their incomes.

Even another income tax indeed would probably not long suffice for the new and enormous
demands of these distant services. Nay, if we
may judge of their expensiveness on so large a
scale, by a reference to the charges of comparatively trivial establishments hitherto maintained
in that quarter, all the remaining resources of
taxation in Great Britain, would scarcely be
able long to supply this vast and unprecedented
drain. The manufactures and agriculture of
this Island, the produce of our Colonies themselves, the rich commerce of the East, and all
the other tributes, which British industry and
enterprise levy through a thousand channels,
from the whole civilized globe, in aid of our national revenue, might be devoted to West India
security, and yet devoted in vain :—numerous,
various, and extensive, though they are, all might
be absorbed in this insatiable gulph, without
lessening the force of its devouring vortex.

    " *Charybdin dico? Oceanus medius fidius*
                            " *vix*

[111]

" *vix videtur, tot res, tam dissipitas, tam dis-*
" *tantibus in locis positas, tam cito, absorbere*
" *potuisse !*"

We might throw the fate of our funds, into
the same scale with that of our Navy; while
France, by merely tossing the sword of negro
freedom, or negro force, into the other, would
make it still preponderate.

I am, Sir, &c. &c

LETTER

LETTER IV.

———

SIR,

OF the task which I prescribed to myself at the outset, one part only, but certainly not the least important, remains to be accomplished.

I have endeavoured to unveil the true nature, and to point out the most probable immediate effects, of the French expedition; and have shewn, though with powers very far inferior to the important work, the new and alarming dangers to which in every possible event of the contest between France and her Colonial Negroes, the Western wing of our Empire will be exposed. It remains to enquire, as I proposed to do in the last place, "*What measures should these prospects suggest, to the prudence of the British Government?*"

If

If our approaching situation in the West Indies is likely to be thus perilous, can that situation be averted by any means in our power to apply? Or if inevitably at hand, is there any preparative measure by which its evils may be palliated?

That we cannot attempt to control the measures which France may think fit to adopt for the government of her Colonies, is sufficiently obvious. To my mind, and I would hope Sir, to your's, it is no less clear, that her hostile or coercive measures ought not to be directly or indirectly assisted by this country; but that we are bound by the plainest rules of policy, if not also in justice towards Toussaint, to observe a strict neutrality. Actively to obstruct the French operations, would be to provoke a new war, but to further them, would only be to hasten, perhaps eventually to augment, the jeopardy of our own Colonies: and were our interference even to produce no worse effect, than that of exciting against us the hatred and enmity of the Negroes, I should regard it as a disadvantage not to be counterbalanced, by the acquisition of a claim on the precarious gratitude of France.

An insidious policy like that which our old enemy practised against us in our quarrel with America, would ill suit the character of Great Britain. Let us disclaim therefore every idea of secretly

fomenting

fomenting or prolonging the impending contest. But let us discern our own interest as well as our duty better, than to assist in hastening its termination. Though the protraction of discord or civil war in Guadaloupe and St. Domingo, is what humanity may regret, it is the best political hope of the British interests in the West Indies. It will postpone at least, the perils of our Leeward Islands and Jamaica, and the call for arduous efforts to defend them. When the labors of the Republic end, our own must immediately commence.

It is not impossible even, that if a sanguinary contest should be long maintained between the Mother Country and her black Colonists, the breach like that between Great Britain and America may grow too wide to be closed, and a final separation may be the issue; and though this would be a case pregnant enough with danger, yet an independent Negro State, would certainly be a less terrible neighbour to the British Sugar Colonies, if irreconcilably hostile to France, than if under her influence, and willing to promote her views.

That the suppression of Negro liberty is not less the cause of Great Britain than of France, is a proposition which our Creole fellow-subjects very naturally wish to maintain; but a British Minister will pause before he admits its truth, and must feel that at least there are sacrifices at the

expence

expence of which that cause ought not to be pro-
moted. He will therefore do well to remember,
that to accelerate the pacification of St. Domingo, would be to place more speedily at the
disposal of the French Government at least
60,000 most formidable troops; to which Guadaloupe and Cayenne would probably add near
20,000 soldiers of the same description; not to
mention the great European force by this time
arrived in the Islands: and it will behove him
to consider what reasonable ground of reliance
we have that this vast force will be afterwards
disbanded, so as not to continue to be a mine
under the foundations of our West India dominion, charged, and ready to be exploded, at the
pleasure of the Republic.

To the planters I admit that invasion will be
less terrible by not bringing enfranchisement in
its rear; but to the British empire at large, it
will be small consolation that the tree of liberty
is not planted along with the tri-coloured standard, if those rich colonies are to be added to
the dominions of an enemy. The evil in a public view, will not be less, by their passing unim-
paired in agricultural wealth, and commercial
importance into the hands of so potent a rival.

Let not self-interested voices then, however
loud, and however specious their representations, prevail upon you to depart from the
straight course of a sincere and exact neutrality

lity. Do not contribute to hasten that perilous
position of our national interests in the West
Indies, which civil war in the French colonies
only can suspend; and which at best will far out-
grow your means of defensive preparation. Let
not the plausible terms of "repressing rebellion,"
"curbing the revolutionary spirit," or whatever
other glosses may be used to disguise the true
nature of the impending contest, induce you
to assist in building a scaffold in the new world,
for that ambition which has already raised so co-
lossal a fabric in the old.

With the moral merits of the question between the two parties, we have no concern; nor
is it clear that did they stand at our judgement
seat, the cause of the Republic would be found
so just, as has been of late industriously represented by some whom dread of negro liberty has
made on this occasion her advocates. But of this
we are certain, that supposing it right in France
to re-establish by her arms, that bondage which
by her laws she abolished, we can have no duty
in the case superior to that of watching over our
own interest and safety: nor is it less clear that
the further extension of her power is an evil, as
much at least to be dreaded, as the independence
or freedom of the negroes; and that therefore as
she can give no effectual security for not using
to our damage her approaching means of annoyance, it would be madness in us to accelerate

a crisis

a crisis that may place them entirely in her hands. In a word, for the re-establishment of order in the French Colonies, we cannot afford to hasten that insecurity of our own which may oblige us to hold them in future, as tenants at will to the Great Nation.

I will insist no further on a point of policy, which with many, may appear too clear to have needed illustration. That you Sir, view it in the same light I shall be happy to discover by your measures; but let me repeat, that a passive line of conduct in his Majesty's Government will probably not suffice to ensure the neutrality of our Colonies; of which the recent aid given to *La-crosse*, in some of our Windward Islands is if report may be credited,* a striking indication.

Of active precautionary measures that may be taken, while the dangers that so awfully threaten our Colonies are yet suspended, I would next briefly speak.

That exterior means of defence can no longer be relied upon as formerly, has I trust been sufficiently shewn. They would be certainly inefficacious; unless provided on a scale much larger than could without ruin to the general interests of the empire be long maintained. But the con-

* Since this sheet was put to press, it is reported that another instance of this kind has occurred at Jamaica; where a bare-faced annulling of recent engagements with Toussaint, is said to have been the first fruits of the notification of Peace with France.

sideration

sideration of expence apart, our Islands could
not in their present state of interior imbecility,
be effectually defended against the new and ever
threatening means of invasion which, in either
of the cases we have contemplated the Republic
would certainly possess, by the arms of the Mother Country alone. Those new powers of hostility, being indigenous in the French Colonies,
would be too abundant and vigorous, to be opposed by the scanty and feeble exotics of European growth, heretofore imported into our own.
To contend with the Republic between the Tropics, without a large portion of the same home-
made belligerent force, would be like beating up
for recruits against Cadmus, who could raise
armies in a moment from the ground.

" Is it necessary then that large bodies of negro
troops, should be raised and maintained in Jamaica and our other Islands ?" If we would long
retain the sovereignty over them ; if we would
prevent their soon swelling the dominions of the
French Republic ; that expedient, objectionable
and hazardous though during the present situation of their brethren in those Islands it may be,
must I think be adopted.

To such a system of defence, were it not a
matter of strict necessity, there are I admit some
serious objections; and the planters, even under
the present circumstances, may be expected pretty
strongly to oppose it. If the enrolling the small
negro force which at an arduous crisis of the late

war

war was very prudently raised, gave general uneasiness in our colonies; how much more would the placing in them permanent garrisons of the same dreaded soldiery, powerful enough to guard against these new dangers of invasion, be a subject of disquietude and alarm! It cannot excite surprize that the white colonists greatly distrust such protectors; between whom and the slaves there must necessarily be the closest sympathy, and often the nearest domestic connections and attachments; for it is impossible that the black soldier should regard the extreme and degrading bondage of his brethren without disgust; nor is it easy to reconcile with that sense of honour inseparable from the profession of arms, and which while it excites, becomes also a necessary check, upon the military spirit, the contempt and abhorrence hitherto attached to the colour of his skin by the people of whom he is to become a defender.

By the colonial politician, it would by no means be thought a trivial objection, that this complexional opprobrium would be lessened; for however absurd and unjust it may appear to European ideas, he approves and cherishes the prejudice; as a wholesome aid to subordination, and a cement of the master's authority. Nor can I in candour affirm, that the existing system, derives no support or security from this source: on the contrary must admit, that had not nature imprinted on the skin of the negro an indelible and striking mark of distinction from his master, or
had

had not prejudice converted it into a badge of
infamy, as well as of servitude, the abrupt and
monstrous disproportion of social condition between the white and black inhabitants of the
colonies, would either not have been formed, or
could not so long have been maintained. But
while we admit, that to create a military order
out of the abject cast, where there are only two
classes of society, divided by the immeasurable
distance between British liberty and the absence
of every social right from each other, would not
be unattended with danger; there is surely room
to hope, that this establishment if successful,
would gradually tend to the peaceable melioration of the social edifice; not only by softening
the prejudices which stand obstinately in the
way of improvement, but by giving such internal means of supporting a vigorous police, as
might lessen the danger of innovation

The ground of *necessity* however is that on
which the plan of defence may best be recommended, and the only one upon which the planters can be expected to accede to it; and if
there be any truth in the remarks which I
have made upon the physical powers of negroes,
opposed to those of Europeans in a hot climate,
it is undeniable that this resort is not only
necessary to save the lives of our soldiers and
seamen, but to attain the end for which they
have been hitherto sacrificed so freely. While
encountered only by the best foreign soldiers of
the

the temperate zone, our brave regiments may be
expected to conquer in any field, however disad-
vantageous, as has recently been proved in
Egypt; but they are men, and must yield to constitutional superiorities so many and so formidable as those with which they would now have
to conflict in West India war; assailed as they
would at the same time be by tropical diseases,
and out-numbered to a fearful excess *.

Since at every step of our progress in this in-
quiry, the extreme and unnatural bondage in
which the great majority of the inhabitants of
those populous Islands is held, presents some
view of danger, or some obstacle to necessary
measures of defence; is there no possibility, it
may be asked, of going to the root of every evil
at once, and strengthening our colonies in the
most effectual way, by interior reformation?

That a reformation of that shocking and opprobrious system is loudly called for, by every
duty which the Christian, or even the philoso-
pher, acknowledges; by every principle which politicians of all parties, or of any party, profess to
hold wise or sacred; is indubitably true. But
unhappily, there has been hitherto no disposi-

* Since these sheets were prepared for the press, I have
heard, to my astonishment, that the black regiments raised
during the war are to be immediately disbanded. If so, it is
a strong proof at once of the prevalence, and the infatuation, of
West India counsels.

tion, and there may now perhaps not be sufficient opportunity, to make it.

There was a time, Sir, and to look back on it may not be useless, when such happy reformation might have been insured. Already I am firmly convinced, its progress would have been great; and a foundation would have been laid, whereupon at this hour of danger a system of interior defence of the most substantial kind might have been speedily and safely erected. I allude to the first efforts made in parliament for an abolition of the slave trade; which I fully agree with its promoters in thinking would have been the surest and easiest mean of correcting all the evils attendant upon West India bondage. Had this great measure been adopted, even at the period limited for it by the votes of the Commons in 1792, very different indeed, would have probably been the present situation of our Islands. Perhaps the day is at hand when this retrospect will furnish an impressive lesson; but it is not yet arrived; and nations, like individuals, seem fated to be taught by experience alone, the inseparable connection between morality and true wisdom.

That the abolition of the slave trade, would now be in time to avert the impending mischief, is more than I venture to affirm, supposing even that in the present temper of parliament it were a measure to be immediately expected. Nor

Nor dare I with any confidence hope, that even
the perilous prospect now opened will lead to
more direct measures of reform; knowing as I do,
how strongly they will be opposed by the private
interests, and even the urgent individual necessities of the planter. For without now entering
upon a subject too wide for incidental discussion
in a work like the present, I must here affirm a
truth, of which though disputed by abolitionists,
the owners of West India estates in general are but
too conscious " that the present large profits of
a successful sugar plantation could not be obtained, if the condition of the slaves were to be
effectually improved."

Would to God that the interest of the master
were really so involved in the well being of the
slave, as has been asserted and admitted in Parliament! With his comparative well-being indeed,
within such varieties as are to be found in the
existing practice, it may and does comport; for
self-interest has certainly by long experience
discovered the lowest degree of subsistence, and
the highest degree of labor, generally consistent with the preservation of life, and the capacity of regular work; and the limits, thus ascertained have formed an average standard of
treatment, from which a master certainly cannot
deviate on the selfish side, without finding by
rapid mortality, and the ruin of his gang, that
his avarice was short-sighted and unwise.
But

But I speak of reformation that is not only to prevent the abuses arising from mistaken selfishness, or from the necessities of indigent masters in particular cases; but to improve the general standard, in point of comfort and happiness; to diminish the ordinary exaction of labor, which is far too great, and to increase the ordinary subsistence, which is far too small, on even the best regulated estates; and it is of such improvements that I reluctantly feel it a duty to say, a due melioration of the lot of the numerous husbandmen would not leave a small West India farm to yield the splendid income it now does to the successful planter*.

But however inveterate, and deeply rooted in that obstinate motive, self-interest, the present practice may be, the extremes to which it has grown cannot I firmly believe, be much longer maintained. Revolution in the French Islands has effected what the abolition of the slave trade might have more happily performed. It has created an indispensable necessity for relaxing the chains of this

---

* The probability and the importance of this fact may not suggest themselves at first sight, to those who are ignorant of the large proportion the number of workmen bears to the extent of the soil in West India husbandry, and of the general mode of their maintenance. One negro to every acre of land is not more than a due proportion, for sugar estates in the old Islands, and they are chiefly fed and clothed by provisions and cloths imported from North America and Europe.

extreme

extreme and brutalizing bondage, and improving
the condition of the slaves.   I will not say
indeed that it is impossible that our planters
should find an alternative; for I believe Buonaparte to be at present a sincere partizan of their
favorite system; and it is perhaps possible, though
very unlikely, that he may be able to arrest the
progress of negro freedom; but between such
improvement, and the holding their plantations
under the dominion of France, they will soon
be driven to choose, Yes Sir, immediate reform
or speedy loss of dominion, is the alternative
now clearly set before us in the West Indies. -
  " But of what nature are the changes which
may effectually correct the evils of the present
system; and that, speedily enough, to substitute
internal strength and security for internal weakness, before the approaching danger arrives?" I
admit that so compleat a reverse is not to be
rapidly effected, without considerable difficulty
and hazard.—Such reformation however, is perhaps not impracticable, if sincerely and earnestly
attempted; and were the present sacrifices essential to such an enterprise to be cordially
made, it might still possibly be crowned with
timely success.
  No such paltry ostensible regulations however, as those with which some West India assemblies have lately amused the English public
will

will be now of any avail! The miserable mockery
of laws whose injunctions no one will enforce,
and the breach of which can be ascertained only
by the offenders themselves, will here produce
no good, except that of convincing the impartial
and considerate how much legislative interposition is needed. The work to be really useful
must go far deeper; and to speak out clearly, the
state of the negroes must be gradually, but fun-
damentally, changed, in all those essential properties of their bondage, but especially in that
dreadful peculiarity of it, to which in the early
part of this address I have called your attention.

While Slaves are not only the absolute, vendible, property of the master, but fed, worked,
and whipped at his discretion, the protection of
the law, were any such sincerely provided, and
any prosecutor found hardy enough to enforce
it, would be like the redress bestowed by the
Knight of La Mancha on the Peasant's boy,
who after that famed avenger of wrongs had
quitted the scene of discipline, was tied up again
to the tree, and expiated together with the first
offence, the more grievous one of having invited
by his cries such dangerous and mortifying interference. Nor is it less apparent that while
these poor Beings are worked under the whip of
the driver, it will be equally vain to attempt to
raise

[127]

raise their characters into a fitness to be governed by municipal laws, or treated like rational agents *.

Of the means by which these great radical evils might be removed, long reflection, aided by a residence of many years in the West Indies has given me some specific ideas; which were there a hope of their being adopted in practice I should feel it a most pleasing labor to unfold. But their development here, while it would swell this long address to a most unreasonable bulk, would I fear be perfectly useless. Till

* More satisfactory confirmation of these opinions cannot be desired than the testimony of the late Mr. Bryan Edwards; who in speaking of the attempt to regulate the exercise of the Master's absolute authority over his slaves by the *Code Noir* of Louis XIV, and of its inefficacy at St. Domingo, assigns these reasons for its failure. " In countries where slavery is " established, the leading principle on which government is " supported is *fear,* or a sense of *that absolute coercive ne-* " *cessity which leaving no choice of action, supersedes all question* " *of right.* It is in vain to deny that such actually is, " and necessarily must be the case of all countries where sla- " very is allowed. Every endeavour therefore *to extend po-* " *sitive rights to men in this state,* as between one class of " people and the other, is *an attempt to reconcile inherent* " *contradictions,* and *to blend principles together which ad-* " *mit not of combination."* (*Hist. of St. Domingo, chap.* 1. *page* 11.) It is scarcely necessary to observe, that by " go- vernment" Mr. Edwards clearly meant the private govern- ment of the Master; and by " absolute-coercive necessity," the coercion of the whip.

some

some disposition is shewn towards reformation
in point of principle, it would be idle to treat of
its details.

That the colonial assemblies will never heartily
set about this interesting work, I am well convinced; and who indeed that knows any thing
of their general composition, or has attended to
the uniform style of their legislation in regard to
negroes, can hope the contrary!—To them however, Parliament has thought it right hitherto
to commit the fate of this large and most helpless body of his Majesty's subjects, (for such, as
they often answer with their lives for breaches
of his laws, I may surely take leave to call
them) and perhaps even the awakening nature
of the present emergency, may not have force
enough to sustain against the clamours of a too
powerful Party, the wisdom of an opposite conduct.

I am aware indeed that the constitutional
right of Parliament to legislate for the Colonies
on this subject, has been denied or questioned in
the House of Commons.

The objection was not less extraordinary, than
a threat or insinuation with which it was said to
have been accompanied, that of resistance by
the white colonists *(risum teneatis?)*—resistance against the Mother Country, whose protection bestowed at an immense expence not
only of treasure but blood, alone can save them
a single

a single day, not only from foreign enemies, but from the continual dangers of that wretched interior system which they so pertinaciously defend!!!—The palsied bed-ridden patient might as rationally threaten violence to his nurse, for putting sustenance into his mouth.

But if the Islands have justice in their claim to exclusive legislation in this case, their imbecility ought not to deprive them of it:—Let us therefore briefly enquire (it may be highly useful at the present juncture to do so) what is the foundation of this pretension?

The power to make laws to bind the Colonies has been constantly exercised by Parliament, from their first settlement, down to the present period; and though the general subjects of such laws, have been navigation, commerce and revenue; yet they have sometimes extended to matters of municipal regulation unconnected with those titles; as for instance, the Stat. 5. Geo. 2. cap. 7. for the more easy recovery of debts.

To such acts of authority no serious objection seems to have been made, till the present Reign; when disputes with the American Colonies arose, from the exercise, not so much of legislative power in general, as from the extending it to the purpose of internal taxation. An Act commonly called the Declaratory Act (6. Geo. 3. cap. 12.) was thereupon made, as a kind of Par-

K   liamentary

liamentary Manifesto, asserting the right to legislate for the Colonies in all cases whatever.

Afterwards, in the year 1778, it was thought
prudent, with a view to conciliation, that this obnoxious Statute should be in some measure coun-
terpoised by the Act 18. Geo. 3. cap. 12.; by
which it is declared, that Parliament will not
impose any tax to be payable in the Colonies,
" except only such as it may be expedient to impose for the regulation of commerce," &c. But
the Declaratory Act, offensive though it had
proved, continued notwithstanding all the trying circumstances of the American contest, and
still continues, unrepealed.—Though the exercise
therefore of the dangerous right of interior
taxation was relinquished by Parliament, even
that sacrifice to Peace was not made, without an
express reservation of the right to impose internal taxes, for certain purposes ; and the latter
Statute does in effect mantain the same general
constitutional right of legislation, in all cases
wherein it is not expressly renounced, that was
universally asserted by the Declaratory Act.

Had Parliament even yielded the exercise of
taxation, not as a voluntary concession to the
Colonial Legislatures, but as an admission of
their exclusive right, to raise internal taxes ; no
sound argument could be drawn from that admission, against the right of legislation in all
other cases. For, as a stout Champion of Colonial

nial Privileges has observed, " there is a material
" distinction between a Power in the Mother
" Country to impose taxes, and a power to make
" laws in general, for the interior government
" of her Colonies ; and the latter may well exist
" without the former."—I cannot quote a better
authority for this distinction, than one which Mr.
Bryan Edwards himself has quoted with approbation—that of the late Lord Chatham ; who is
cited as having used the following words, "Taxa-
" tion is no part of the governing or legislative
" power. Taxes are a voluntary gift and grant of
" the Commons alone. In legislation, the three
" Estates of the Realm are alike concerned; but
" the concurrence of the Peers and the Crown
" to a tax, is only necessary to clothe it in the
" form of a law. The gift and grant is of
" the Commons alone *. The Declaratory
Act therefore is not only unrepealed, but unim-
peached in its general principle, by the utmost
concession that the pressure of public difficulties during the American quarrel could extort.

Nor was this celebrated Act the first that generally and broadly asserted the right in question; for I cannot conceive a clearer or more
emphatic declaration of it than is contained in
the 7th and 8th Will. III. cap. 22. sec. 9; whereby

* _History of the West Indies, by Mr. B. Edwards, vol._ ii. 365,

all

all laws made in the colonies, repugnant to English statutes extending to or naming them, are declared to be void.

While such statutes remain unrepealed, I am at a loss to conceive how this right, exercised as it has been in numberless instances, from the very first settlement of our Colonies, and as well subsequently to, as before, the independency of North America, can be decently questioned in Parliament. Yet if newspaper reports may be relied upon, it not only has been denied by some advocates for the Slave Trade in the House of Commons, but men high in office have deprecated its discussion as the "*stirring of a delicate constitutional question ! ! !*" If so important a right was thought too much to renounce for the preservation of America, and to the Assemblies of the great continental Colonies; but was asserted and maintained to the end, in the face of rebellion; it seems strange that complaisance to the petty legislatures of the Sugar Islands, should now lead a Statesman to speak of it in Parliament as a matter liable to. doubt.

Were it not for the undue consequence that such language, if really uttered, may have given to this strange claim of exclusive authority in the Assemblies, I should not think it worthy of further remark : but were there room

for

for doubt, it would perhaps be conclusive to say, that the great principle upon which the North American Colonies asserted their exclusive right to interior legislation, does not fairly apply to the case which we are considering; that of a law to MELIORATE THE CONDITION OF THE SLAVES.

The least resistible argument on the part of the Americans, was, that as they were not represented in the British Parliament, and the members of that Assembly would not themselves be bound by the laws which they might frame for America, the being subjected to the unlimited authority of the legislature of the Mother Country, would bereave the Colonists of the only security the unrepresented have against oppression; that of the law makers, being no less than their actual or virtual electors, subject in general to the same municipal duties or restraints which they may impose on the rest of the community. But this consideration, if applied to the great mass of the population of our Islands, the slaves, will be found so far from warranting the same practical conclusion, that it will make the absurdity, as well as injustice, of excluding in favour of their masters the legislative authority of Parliament, abundantly evident. Are the enslaved negroes represented in the colonial assemblies? or are the members of those bodies or their constituents subject to the same laws by which

which this great class of the community is governed? Are not those Legislators, on the contrary, men who upon all questions touching the
private relation of master and slave, are interested parties; and who are even inversely to be
affected by the proposed law, instead of being
in the same manner subject to it; since privilege
to the slaves must necessarily in the same degree be restraint upon the master; and fresh re-
traint on them, were there room for it, increase
of his authority?

The West India Assemblies then would claim
this concession denied to North America, in direct opposition to the great principle of reason and
justice on which it was in that case demanded.
They would be exclusive Legislators upon this
subject, though they are emphatically liable to
the very same objection, on account of which the
general concurrent legislation of Parliament in
the Colonies was most plausibly opposed.

It cannot here be fairly replied, " that the civil
character of the slave is absorbed in that of the
master, by whom therefore he is sufficiently represented." For the question supposes, that for the
purposes under consideration at least, he is intitled to the protection of laws against the
master himself; and the supposed doubt only is,
by whom those laws should be made. So far
therefore as this right extends, his civil character
is not merged in, but must be considered as distinct

tinct, from that of the master. He is admitted so
far to have claims on the legislative power of the
State; and the single question is whether Parliament is bound by constitutional principle, to
refer those claims to an assembly of masters, in
derogation of whose absolute authority they are
advanced. I maintain therefore Sir, that were
this claim of exemption from the authority of
Parliament as well founded as it is obviously the
reverse, the case of the slaves ought to form an
exception to it.

That the Imperial Legislature has an incontestable right to make laws for the government
of the Colonies, in some cases at least, is admitted even by those who dispute the universality of
that right the most strenuously. " The Colonies
(says Mr. B. Edwards *) " readily admit they
" stand towards the British Legislature, in the
" degree of subordination, which implies every
" authority in the latter, essential to the pre-
" servation of the whole ; and to the mainte-
" nance of the relation between a Mother Coun-
" try and her Colonies." And the same author
admits, that this constitutional right is not limited by any known or general boundaries ; but
depends upon the nature of the particular circumstances that may call for its exertion. " To
" ascertain (says he) " the various contingen-

* History of the West Indies, vol. ii. 361. 2.

" cies

" cies, and circumstances, wherein, on the prin-
" ciples stated, the British Legislature has, and
" has not, a right to interpose, is perhaps im-
" possible; because circumstances may occur to
" render its interposition necessary which can-
" not be foreseen;"* and he cites Governor
Pownall's opinion to the same effect.

Upon such concessions, unwilling and sparing
though they are, the right of Parliamentary interposition to reform the system of slavery, cannot well be denied; for first, we have in this case
an emergency of no trivial kind; and such as
might well justify the exercise of a superintend-
ing power reserved for difficult and extraordinary occasions. If to redress the wrongs, or meliorate the deplorable condition, of seven-eighths
of his Majesty's subjects in the Sugar Colonies,
when both reason and experience demonstrate
they have no relief to expect from the Assemblies, and when their hard lot is not without some
colour of reason ascribed to Parliament itself†
be not a purpose weighty and necessary enough
to

* History of the West Indies, vol. ii. 365.

† Of the Legislative sanction given by Great Britain to
the slave trade the anti-abolitionists have made great use;
and it has been hastily inferred that the bondage of the Colonies has received the stamp of the same authority; but the
fact seems to be, that Parliament till the present æra, never
enquired into what state the African exiles of which it authorised

to justify such an interposition, I am at a loss
to fancy any circumstances that would in this
view sanction the exercise of this acknowledged
extraordinary power. If this be not really
" dignus vindice nodus," let a stronger case be
defined. But secondly, here is also a case in
which the Mother Country has herself a most
important and direct interest, in the proposed
subject of legislation; and not only so, but to
use Mr. Edwards's words, the reformation in
question is become necessary " to the preservation of the whole common interest," and to
the "maintenance of that relation" which sub-
sists between Great Britain and these Colonies:
for that his Majesty's sovereignty over them is
endangered by the present condition of the
slaves, in consequence of the new situation of the
French Colonies, has I trust been demonstrated;
nor is it less clear that the Mother Country has
an interest in correcting abuses of which the
effects must fall with a most grievous pressure

rised the deportation, were carried. From the colonial acts
of assembly no such information could be obtained; for however surprising it may appear, no positive law has introduced
or defined this strange and unprecedented relation between
master and slave; but its legality wholly rests, in all the Colonies I am acquainted with, on a kind of lex non scripta, or
custom, founded in the rudest period of their history, by the
barbarous Buccaneers who first settled the oldest of our West
India Islands.

on the revenue and defensive resources of the empire.

Indeed Sir, when I regard the force of the latter consideration, it seems hardly to be apprehended that the objection I am combating will ever again be advanced; for surely the experience of the late war has sufficiently proved had it been doubtful before, that of a bad interior system in our Colonies the penalties must chiefly be borne by those who are represented in the Imperial Parliament. What, during the late arduous contest, or at least after its two first campaigns, so fatally diverted our efforts from European to trans-Atlantic War, but the insecurity of our West India Islands? And by what were they chiefly endangered but their own bad interior policy? There was I admit conflagration in their neighbourhood, but the peril chiefly arose from their own combustible texture. Except a few miserable privateers, a hostile flag was scarcely to be seen in their seas; and the governments of the French Colonies were not in circumstances to attempt invasion on any but the minutest scale. If a few boats full of negroes were sent by Hugues to Dominique, St. Vincents and Grenada, that was the utmost extent of his offensive efforts; and yet, what an enormous diversion of British force was long produced by them! With how much of our bravest blood, not indeed shed by the sword, but fatally polluted by disease, were these

these contemptible sparks extinguished! Had not the great mass of the people in our Islands been in a state that precluded all hope of fidelity, the smallest of those colonies might have bidden defiance to such feeble powers of invasion as the enemy possessed.

Nor can it be said, that this was a peculiar situation not likely to recur; unless all the premises opened in a former part of this address can be denied; or unless it can be demonstrated that the infant Hercules of negro liberty will be effectually slaughtered in his cradle. On the contrary, it has been proved that the weakness of our own Colonial system, is likely to be contrasted by hostile energies still more powerful in every future war.

Should then Sir, this essential right of legislation be still denied; should none of the other considerations I have urged, suffice to silence self-interested objectors, I would produce to them the enormous returns of mortality in our fleets and armies; with the equally enormous accounts of West India expenditure; and bid them read there the title deeds of this Parliamentary authority. If more were still wanting, I would request them to read the St. Vincent and Grenada Loan Acts, now recently renewed, and to calculate how much must be ultimately lost to the nation, and how much was added to the public burthens, by raising at a most critical

and

and distressful period, the millions thereby lent to repair the effects of insurrection.

It would be monstrous to maintain that the Mother Country has no right to correct by wholesome laws, evils by which she is exposed to such costly demands for protection and relief. It would be to say, that the planter has a right to raise and maintain at pleasure on his own land a nuisance pestiferous to the vital resources of the empire; and that Parliament has no right to enter and abate it. Nay more, that the Mother Country is bound to be his insurer against his private share of the damage that may ensue from his own wrong. Unless all this is to be conceded, or in other words, unless the political relation is to be reversed, the Mother Country to become dependent on the Colonies, and the people of England to hold their power and wealth at the will of West India Assemblies, you have a right to regulate the weight of those costly chains, the stuff to repair which must be your gold, and the anvils the keels of your navy.

Perhaps there are some, who admitting the Parliamentary right to be incontestable, may question whether the exercise of it will be expedient; and may be disposed to say "the Insular Assemblies best know the nature of the disease, and how to apply the remedy."

Their superiority of judgement on the subject I will admit when it shall be proved to me that

prejudice

prejudice and self-interest are, less unfriendly to fair inference, than local distance from the facts in question. But the wisdom of our laws has not unfrequently proceeded upon a different principle; as for example, when their favourite mode of investigating truth by a jury of the vicinage is broken through, on account of popular prejudices or partiality, in the hundred or county. I will not pay our West India fellow subjects the compliment of saying that they are fitter for impartial deliberations, while under the bias of real or imagined self-interest, than a jury of Englishmen. And were it reasonable to give them such a preference in any case, the slightest knowledge of their laws would forbid the allowance of it in the present.

Take into your hands Sir, the volumes of Acts of Assembly of the different West India Islands; and where you find "negroes" or "slaves" in the index, refer to the Acts that relate to them. Till within the last few years, you will not find in a century or more, a single provision in these laws tending to protect a class of men by far the most numerous in those societies, from the injuries to which their situation must always have exposed them: not one clause to limit the master's authority; not one to punish its abuse. With the exception of a provision or two in some of the Islands, against murder or maiming, I recollect no instance of any law to protect

the

the slave against the severity of the worst of owners; much less to guard him against those more general and important sufferings, to which his absolute dependence, especially upon an avaricious or indigent master, obviously subjected him, in the articles of labour and food.

Yet the slaves have been by no means forgotten by these local legislatures. You will find them on the contrary to have been a very frequent subject of attention : but where their name occurs in the outset of a section, you will be sure to find stripes or death at the end of it.

That these poor bondsmen stood not in need of laws to protect, as well as to punish them, will hardly be supposed, even by the least considerate. The recent laws of many of the Islands would alone serve to prove incontestably the reverse. For *since the subject of West India slavery has been brought so much under the notice of the English public, and of Parliament*, Acts of Assembly have been passed, professing to control in some very essential points, especially in regard to the measure of food and of labour, the master's before unlimited discretion.

But while such laws manifest the grossness of former neglect, I am sorry to say that they prove no genuine change of character in the colonial legislatures. For no man possessed of the smallest knowledge of the subject, can consider them, without perceiving not only their utter inade-

quacy

quacy to the ends proposed, but the impossibility that their provisions, such as they in general are, can be enforced. What their effects in Jamaica have been indeed, I know not from any direct information : but am authorised to affirm, that at the Leeward Islands at least, these new Acts are a mere dead letter; and that not an instance has occurred, in those Islands hitherto, of any attempt to enforce them. I should be much surprised to see the record of a single conviction upon them produced from any part of the West Indies; and if that cannot be done, several years after the enactment of such novel laws, and upon so extensive a subject, the conclusion is sufficiently obvious.

Should Parliament decline the exercise of a concurrent legislation from confidence in these Assemblies, it would form a strong contrast with its jealousy of them in other cases; where the cause of distrust is less weighty. When the colonial purse of the Crown, or the interests of navigation, are concerned, there has not been left to them even a concurrent power, of making laws for their own internal government.

Various, and formidable, are the powers to be exercised in the colonies by naval and revenue officers under many acts of parliament : and they are not rarely of a kind that seems peculiarly to require the regulation or control of

some

some authority nearer than Europe* yet by
Stat. 7. & 8. Will. III. Cap. 22. Sec. 9. "all laws,
" by-laws, usages, or customs in the colonies,
" against the provisions of that or any other act
" of parliament extending to them" are expressly declared to be void. Nay more, the execution of these laws is not entrusted to the ordinary courts of the colony, formed upon the model
of those at Westminster, and proceeding by a
course known to the constitution of England;
but the jurisdiction is given to courts of admiralty; in which a single judge, appointed by the
Crown, and holding his office at the royal will,
decides both on the law and the fact without the
intervention of a jury †.

What Sir, is the reason, or the apology, for such
an exclusive legislature in these cases; exercised
as it has been without complaint, in a variety of
cases, even since the repeal of the Declaratory Act,
and aided by such an inroad upon general British
privileges? Distrust of the Assemblies; and of
the ordinary courts and juries of these Islands;
on account of their *particular interests,* and on
account of their *prejudices* against those wholesome restraints on their trade, which the parent

* See 13. and 14. Car. II. Cap. 11, and 7. and 8. Will. III.
Cap. 22. Sec. 6.

† See Stat. 22. and 23. Car. II. Cap. 26, Sec. 12. 4 Gco. III.
Cap. 15, Sec. 41.

state

state for the common benefit thinks necessary to maintain.

Such power is exercised without scruple from regard to the public revenue, or even to the private merchants of this country; as in the Stat. 5. Geo. II. cap. 7. which for the easier recovery of debts in the colonies due to individuals here, makes an ex parte affidavit sent from England, equivalent in their courts to a viva voce examination of witnesses between the parties *.

But

---

* This Statute also provided that lands and other real estate and negroes in the colonies should be liable to the simple contract debts of the owner, and might be taken in execution and sold in the same manner as personal estates. Upon the injustice and cruelty of these provisions in respect of the slaves, Mr. B. Edwards took occasion in his History of Jamaica, to remark very strongly, and to arraign the abolitionists of inconsistency and want of feeling in not moving for their repeal in parliament. The negroes, he observed, were liable to be dragged from the estate on which they and their families were established, and from all those little sources of comfort dependent on the soil, which good conduct and industry might have obtained for them ; to be separated from their wives and children; to be sold to a stranger ; perhaps carried into a foreign land to end a miserable existence: and to be thus persecuted because the master was unfortunate ! *(see the very pathetic passage in his History of the West Indies, vol. ii. cap. 4. page 154.)* He adds " that the hard case is " one that occurs in practice every day: that the statute " was disgraceful to the national character and to huma- " nity and that it ought to be repealed ; and suggests, that the " negroes ought to be attached to the land and sold with it."

L   Upon

But when the reformation of a rank and inveterate system of evils, built up and cherished by
the

Upon these principles, Mr. Edwards, in the year 1797,
brought into parliament, a bill which passed into a law
(see 37. Geo. III. cap. 119.) with no small eclat to West India
humanity ; and discredit to the comparative negligence of abolitionists. And how did this benevolent measure remedy the
evil ? *Why by repealing the Statute 5. Geo. II. Cap. 7. as to
the* NEGROES, *but leaving it in force* AS TO THE LAND. i. e. *To.
prevent the negroes from being torn from the estate they belong
to, the estate alone is to change masters; and they can no longer
be sold along with it,* as was notoriously the former course of
proceeding when plantation negroes were sold under executions
at law !!! They must therefore not only quit their houses,
provision grounds, and other local comforts, with such of their
wives and children as belong to neighbouring estates ; but must
follow the fortunes of an insolvent master, who has no longer an
estate on which to place them ; and who must consequently either
hire them out to a stranger, a plan peculiarly hostile to their
welfare ; or transport them to settle new lands in some foreign
territory, and divide them from all the objects of their early
attachments for ever !!

Such is the humanity and wisdom of this boasted Act ! the
single boon of parliament to a hapless race to whose industry
the nation owes so much, and who have such strong claims on
legislative protection !!! But let the English reader be relieved ! No harm I can assure him has been actually done by
this Statute; which is so strangely at variance with its
own principle. The truth is, that long prior to the Act
5. Geo. II. the local laws of every West India colony we then
possessed, had made slaves liable to executions at law; and
that not generally, or with the land, but expressly *in pri-
ority to the plantation and other real estate* of the owner to
whom

the Colonial Assemblies themselves; a reformation which so many motives of justice, humanity,

whom they belonged : and in every Island that we have acquired since that Statute was made, Acts of Assembly have been
passed, adopting in this respect the laws of the older colonies.
By their express provisions, and by the very words of their
writ of execution, land cannot be seized or sold, but in default
of slaves of value enough to satisfy the debt: so that the barbarous consequences pointed out by Mr. B. Edwards would
uniformly arise, were it not that the natural progress of in-
solvency among planters, provides a security against them.
Fortunately, long before an estate is taken in execution, the
land and slaves are generally deeply mortgaged together, and
the equity of redemption of both is sold in such cases, in one
lot, to preserve the rights of the mortgagee; who is also
commonly in possession before a sale under an execution takes
place ; and as commonly is himself the purchaser of the equity
of redemption.

The truth therefore is, that though West India estates are
very frequently sold by executions at law, the cruel effects
pointed out by Mr. Edwards are by no means so frequent as
he represented when he was thus loading the British Parliament with the sins of the Insular legislatures.

I ought in justice to that writer, who I am sorry to find is
now removed from the lists of human controversy, to observe,
that he has himself, in page 153 of the book last cited, admitted the grievance in question not to have been *originally
created* by parliament; but I wish he had been more explicit,
and shewn that existing Acts of Assembly were in truth the
only operative laws on the subject. I lament that he is not
now living, to contradict or admit the assertion " that notwithstanding his strong reprobation of this part of the Insular
law,

nity, and sound policy, demand from us, is in question; Parliament, far from claiming the sole authority, is to forego, it seems, even the exercise of a concurrent power; and on the prayer of the poor negroes for that interposition which is their only hope, is to say to these Assemblies

> ————" Come cousin Angelo,
> " In this I'll be impartial, be you judge
> " Of your own cause!!"

If the Insular Assemblies even had the best inclination, to reform the interior system, they are not independent enough of the popular voice, in those small communities in the bosoms whereof they sit, to do their duty in this very important branch of legislation. Could a majority of enlightened men exempt from those prejudices by which ancient and general abuses are supported, be found in those representa-

law, and the general assent given to his opinions by the West India interest in Parliament, while his bill was in its progress, *not one of those Acts of Assembly has yet been repealed or altered.* That executions at law are not rarely a source of extreme injustice and cruelty to the human objects of sale, is undeniable; though not so often in the case of plantation slaves as Mr. Edwards supposed; but in general there is a much greater calamity incident to their unhappy state than being sold from an insolvent master; and West Indians will feel the force of my meaning, when I add " *it is the not being sold soon enough.*"

tive

tive bodies; yet no man I am sure who knows the West Indies, or who has perused the volume of human nature any where, will suppose the constituents in general, much less the general body of free inhabitants, to be of the same character. Speaking from experience, I hesitate not to affirm, that there is on the contrary as strong vehement and obstinate a popular attachment to all the extreme powers of the master in the West Indies, as the most free and high-spirited people in Europe ever manifested for their ancient constitutional rights.

When therefore it is considered how closely in these small societies, an Assembly man must be drawn into contact with his electors, and the free colonists at large; and how the momentous difference of complexion has there eclipsed almost every other distinction, placing all white men not in servile situations, nearly upon a par, the difficulty of such legislators effectually opposing themselves to the sense of the multitude, will be pretty apparent. That they should attempt to do so, it would be vain to expect; that they should have courage to persevere, is still more hopeless.

To such mere pretexts of reformation as the recent laws to which I have alluded, little indeed, if any, popular opposition may have been raised; for their want of practical force, as well as their utility in answering a certain purpose in this

Country,

Country, was pretty generally understood; and masters knew that they might laugh at the rod without a hand with which they were menaced, even had it not been a rod of feathers. But should the Assemblies begin in earnest to control the authority of the master, and improve the condition of the slave, by provisions really operative, and sanctions of which the strength should be proportioned to the difficulties of bringing them home to offenders; I know enough of West India communities to affirm that the law-makers would stand in need of the firmness of martyrs, and would possibly have to meet their fate.

But the Assemblies will never put the temper of their constituents to so severe a trial. They are themselves masters; and the ulcer will be tenderly touched, when the incision knife is in the hand of the patient.

The foundation then, Sir, on which alone I deem it practicable to build the future security of the sugar Colonies, is that of meliorating the condition of the great mass of the people, and converting them from dangerous enemies into defenders, and this is only to be done by the exercise of the Legislative Authority of Parliament. If through mistaken principles, of policy, or deference for an active and powerful party, that right, and let me also call it that duty, shall be still neglected, the slave system will continue to be a source of internal weakness and danger till

revolution

revolution or foreign conquest become the well merited result.

Till Parliament shall resolve to enter upon this great and necessary work, it would be vain to propose specific plans either of interior defence or reformation; as they would certainly either not be adopted by the Assemblies, or be adopted only in such an elusory manner as to frustrate the intended effect. The preceding general hints therefore are the whole that I shall for the present offer to your attention. When an efficient moving power shall be obtained, it will be time enough to consider how the parts of the machine may be best constructed and applied.

There remains one very important and leading object of this address, to which I have hitherto forborn to advert.

To the West India possessions of Great Britain the Peace has now made a great and very valuable addition. The large and fertile Island of Trinidada, an Island comprising perhaps 1500 square miles of the richest territory between the tropics, has been added to the crown of the United Kingdoms.

" What a mine of wealth has Spanish indo-
" lence left unopened in this luxuriant soil, of
" which scarcely a thousandth part perhaps has
" yet

" yet been put in tillage, nor one acre in a hun-
" dred yet granted from the crown!* What
" large sums may be raised by the sale of these
" lands! and what great additions made by their
" future produce to our imports and revenue!
" Let Trinidada only be placed on the same
" footing, in point of constitution and laws, with
" our other West India Colonies, and her ports
" be open to the slave trade; and British enter-
" prise will soon realise these golden prospects.
" The uncleared lands will be purchased at high
" prices, by eager competitors; they will soon
" be disencumbered of their timber, thrown open
" to the sun, and broken by the hoe; the sugar
" cane will speedily cover with its most luxu-
" riant growth the whole surface of the Island;
" and the produce will equal, if not exceed,
" the most abundant crops of Jamaica!"

Such are the dreams of avarice, and such already has been the language which she has insi-
nuated not only into the public mind, but I doubt
not also still more assiduously, into your own pri-

* I have taken some pains to obtain accurate accounts of
the extent both of the settled and unsettled lands of Trinidada,
and the present state of its population and produce; but have
found it very difficult to procure such information as might be
depended upon. Since official accounts of all those particulars
are very soon to be laid before Parliament and, will no doubt
speedily be published, I forbear to offer the less satisfactory
results of private enquiries.

vate

vate ear. But from the delusions of these wizard scenes, let the considerations here set before you be your safeguard; for if they have any force, those gaudy prospects have no more reality, than the verdant fields which tempt the feverish patient in a calenture to plunge into the ocean.

That you have the means of immediately opening a new slave Colony of great agricultural capacity, is indeed true; nor can it be denied that commercial enterprise would probably make rapid advances in its settlement. Open the flood-gates of the Guinea market upon this new soil, and it will soon be saturated with many millions of British capital spent in improvements; but before you plant, it is prudent to enquire who is likely to reap the harvest. Before any proportionate returns for this great capital can be expected, the perilous crisis which we have been contemplating, will most probably arrive; and then if your old Colonies are to be in jeopardy, let us enquire what better security will you have in the new?

Wherever negro bondage is planted, interior danger and imbecility must inevitably take root with it; and grow with its growth; but this must more especially be the case, where an extensive Island is rapidly peopled with new negroes from Africa; because, it is an admitted fact, that such negroes are far more prone to insurrection than the Creole slave, who is subdued

by

byeducation to his degraded state, and is rendered
by habit less intolerant of the yoke; because also,
numbers, and a wide range of territory, give confidence to the spirit of revolt; and because, the
dreadful mortality, ever attendant on the clearing
of new lands between the tropics, must form one
great additional subject of discontent. When it is
considered that no Island comparable in magnitude to Trinadada, has yet been settled with the
rapidity which from the present extent of credit,
and prevalence of West India speculation, may
in this case be expected, these interior sources of
weakness and insecurity seem likely to be great
there beyond all former precedent. Nor should it
be forgotten that the shock to commercial credit from the loss of such a Colony, would be
dangerous, in proportion to the recency and
magnitude of the speculations of which it had
been the field.

If we look to the exterior sources of danger,
we shall find that Trinidada will be exposed
beyond most of our other Islands to invasion; while in the case supposed, it would present the strongest attractions to an enemy. It
has the important disadvantage in a belligerent
view, of being situated to leeward of Cayenne
and of all the Dutch Settlements on the Continent, within a short distance from the former,
and still nearer to all the latter; and is separated on the South only by a narrow straight,

from

from the Spanish main; while Tobago, an Island now restored to the Republic, lies close to its opposite shore. By Colonies therefore either of France, or of Powers dependent upon France, this Island is in a manner surrounded, and from thence at all times accessible.

The situation in respect of those powers strongly resembles that of Great Britain itself since the late conquests of France; but to improve the likeness, we must suppose that power, or her dependents, possessed not only of the whole coast of the northern ocean, to the furthest extremity of Norway, but also of Ireland; and the wind perpetually to blow from the greater part of those shores upon our own. The case of Trinidada would even be one of still greater exposure; because the defensive resources of Great Britain are chiefly internal, and her fleet might be easily collected on the coast which she would have to guard; whereas Trinidada could scarcely rely on the timely aid of any other military or naval force, than that which might be at all times appropriated to the object of its single defence, and which might be taken out of the general scale of West India war for the purpose. We have restored Martinico; and long before ships could turn up to the gulph of Paria, with reinforcements from the Leeward Island station, the issue of invasion must be decided.

It is however from the new political circumstances

stances of the French Colonies that these geographical ones would derive their most formidable importance. We have seen that Cayenne is one of the settlements in which revolution has given to France a negro army, together with other advantages quite incalculable when opposed to our own wretched colonial system, unless counter-revolution shall have reversed the free condition of the people. She must, it has been further shewn, if unwise enough even to abandon a reformation so useful and so wholly innoxious as has been effected in this Colony, become very formidable to a hostile neighbour by the great military establishment which will be necessary to enforce and maintain submission; and which, however ineffecual to secure permanently domestic peace, will be a ready weapon of offence against an enemy that lies at the threshold.

While either the energies of negro freedom, or a force equal to its permanent subversion, will continually threaten from this quarter; the great extension of the limits of French Guyana, by the late cession of Portugal, if not relinquished by the Republic, will by enlarging the population and the defensive establishments of the province, increase the power of annoyance. But should France still want a force adequate to the conquest of Trinidada, she would have auxiliaries enough at hand. From the Dutch garrisons of Surinam, Demerara, Berbice,

Berbice, and Isequibo, draughts would hardly
be refused at the instance of the Great Nation,
for an object which forty-eight hours might ac-
complish. Nor is it probable that the government of the Caraccas, would inflexibly deny its
assistance, in an enterprise from which Spain
might obtain revenge, if not restitution.

I entreat you, Sir, to weigh well these considerations, and those offered in my former letters, before you suffer twenty or thirty millions of
British capital to rush into the soil of Trinidada, and tempt the cupidity of France *. To
found a new slave Colony in that neighbourhood, seems to me scarcely less irrational, than
it would be to build a town near the crater of
Vesuvius.

If the wealth of this country be so redundant,
that a waste like this is desirable for its own
sake, like a hemorrhage to a plethoric patient;
or the Slave Trade so hallowed a business, as to
be followed like loyalty or devotion, for its own
sake, "whether we win or lose the game," yet
Sir I conjure you to pause in this case for the
sake of our old sugar Colonies.

And here I call upon the planters of Jamaica,
and the other Islands, though to some of the

* This will hardly appear an excessive estimate, if it be
true that above 18 millions were laid out by British subjects
in Dutch Guyana, while we held it by the short and uncertain
tenure of the sword.

principles

principles professed in this address they may be reasonably supposed inimical, to join in the deprecating a measure to them so pernicious and fatal, as the immediate settlement of this large Island upon the system hitherto pursued.

I here resort not to arguments, which however specious, and however sound, I know will never induce them to coalesce with any opposition to the Slave Trade. No possible advance in the price of negroes, or depreciation of West India produce, are to them evils half so unwelcome, as the slightest victory the friends of Africa might gain upon abolition principles; as was sufficiently witnessed by their silent acquiescence in some late measures of government. While they strenuously and successfully opposed a suppression of this commerce upon an almost exhausted part of the coast of Africa, from which they admitted the supply to be an object of no moment, they saw without an audible murmur, three-fourths of the whole existing Slave Trade of this country poured into the conquered Colonies, to open new lands there upon British account, and raise by their future produce a powerful rivalship in the sugar and cotton markets of Europe.

Against prejudices like these Sir, I know it would be vain to contend. I would as soon undertake to convince the dealers in the Slave Trade and their advocates, that the particular
interests

interests of Liverpool should yield when opposed to those of the empire at large. But I
conjure the planters to consider, that it is possible a crisis may have arrived, when the preservation of their estates, or at least of the British
character of their estates, may depend upon
such a change of system as unluckily falls in
with the odious views of abolitionists; and
coolly to enquire, whether the present be not
such a crisis.

They well know how to appreciate the difficulties of defensive West India war, in circumstances like those in which we are likely soon to be
placed. Making even every allowance which
their most flattering hopes can suggest, for a
possible aggravation of the approaching dangers in the views I have laid before you, they
must at least feel that the defence of our West
India dominions will in future be a most arduous duty ; and they must know that the efforts of the nation, though great, cannot be
unlimited. Let them therefore fairly weigh
the effects of such a diversion of force as
must arise from the importance and great vul-
nerability of Trinidada, if now to be settled
by the Slave Trade.

They need not to be told that a naval or military force at Jamaica would scarcely be any
greater security to that distant windward Island,
than the troops quartered at Colchester, or the
ships

ships in ordinary at Portsmouth. Nor, though it may not be so obvious to European ideas, would the force stationed in the Leeward Islands be less incapable of bringing timely succour to prevent invasion or conquest. The course of the trade wind among those Islands, much more than their local proximity or distance, fixes the effects of their relative positions for the purposes of war.

From the interposition of that great naval arsenal of France, Martinique, and of the now very powerful Colony of Guadaloupe, between our Leeward Island station and Trinidada, the necessity of maintaining distinct defensive establishments at both the latter might be more clearly demonstrated. But it would be a waste of time to insist further upon propositions so clear, as that a force independent of all our other defensive establishments in the same quarter of the world, must be maintained in the gulph of Paria, proportionate to the importance of this new Island, and the danger of its situation; and that this peculiar and necessary service must greatly impair the means by which the old Colonies might in the approaching crisis hope to be defended.

Look back, Sir, on what has been formerly observed respecting the waste of life and of treasure in West India wars. Then while you contemplate the addition of this new branch of service, consider also its probable magnitude, from the great extent

extent of the Island, the facility of invasion, and the greatness of the hostile force by which it will be surrounded. Reflect next, on the great sickliness, to which in common with all lands in that climate while under the process of clearing, this Island is undeniably subject, and to which its brave defenders would consequently in a high degree be exposed; and then say, whether the suggestions of avarice are not contrary to the dictates of sound policy, on this momentous occasion!

Should it after all be thought too much to desist finally from the extension of our cart-whip empire, and the enlargement of our once repudiated Slave Trade, in the settlement of this new Colony, at least let the rash measure be postponed. Let us wait till the storm shall have subsided before we send to sea a new and richly freighted bottom.

If the produce of the sale of the Crown lands be a temptation which the national wisdom and justice cannot wholly resist, let avarice at least not ruin her own object by a foolish impetuosity. In any event of the French West India enterprise that can at all weaken the force of these remarks, the vacant lands will certainly sell to much greater profit than at the present period, while negro freedom is yet unsubdued, and immense negro armies unconquered and undisbanded. The alarming prosM   pects

pects I have set before you, will probably soon
be brought nearer to the eye if real, or dissi-
pated if delusive. Does the Chief Consul really
mean, as he promises, to maintain negro freedom
at Guadaloupe and St. Domingo? His first measures there will probably prove that intention;
and then who will assert it to be prudent in
Great Britain to found new Colonies of
slaves? If on the contrary, his views have been
rightly delineated in the former part of this address, the resistance he may immediately experience will possibly demonstrate in a short time
the extreme difficulty of the enterprise; and
prove to every thinking mind, that either his
final defeat, or a compromise with negro liberty
highly dangerous to our Colonies, or the maintenance of enormous military establishments,
to us, in a national view not less dangerous,
must be the ultimate result: in either of these
cases, my practical conclusion must be abundantly clear.

The only possible event which can make the
planting of the old system in this new soil, less
than political phrenzy, is that of an easy, total,
lasting, counter-revolution in those Colonies, by
which the old bondage shall be there essentially
and permanently restored. Of this result, the
proof cannot, I admit, be so speedy; for the utmost apparent success on the arrival of the armament, will not, as before remarked, be a sure
advance

advance towards the ultimate object. In this case therefore, it is true that you will have to wait till the drivers shall have resumed their former occupation, till labour shall, for a short period at least, have again been peaceably pursued under the coercing whip; and above all, till the Republic shall disband her negro armies, and reduce her European force in the Colonies, within limits approaching to the par of her former establishments, and consistent with the safety of her neighbours.

Even this longest term of suspense however might be patiently endured, if avarice would but fairly calculate the improvements of the future proceeds of the sales of unsettled lands, when an experiment so decisive, shall have proved the dreaded progress of negro emancipation to be for ever defeated. Mean time every substantial advance towards this consummation of the planter's wishes, will render the measure which I deprecate less indefensible in point of policy, and the sale of the Crown lands less wasteful.

Let it not be for a moment understood, that to plead for mere delay, is the whole extent of my purpose; or that I despair of a more enlarged and generous policy being successfully recommended to you, Sir, and to your colleagues in administration. I hope the arguments which have been offered, and the stronger ones which might upon moral principles be adduced,

duced, will suffice to obtain for Africa in this case more than a respite.

But it has gone abroad, I know not on what authority, that an immediate sale of the Crown lands in Trinidada was a measure actually in the contemplation of his Majesty's Ministers; and it is obvious, that such sales if now made, would be pledges from government to the purchasers, for the admission of slavery and of the Slave Trade. It is added, that when against this bold and bad measure the security of an official declaration was desired by a highly respectable Member of the House of Commons, you declined publicly to engage for even the suspension of such sales till the wisdom of Parliament should deliberate on the important subject.

Pardon me, Sir, if the effect in my mind of such reports, has been an injurious distrust of your intentions in this most momentous affair. Nothing but the great prevalence of such rumours, and the recent triumphs of Slave Trade interests over the clearest dictates of sound national policy, could have made me apprehend the possibility of a new Slave Colony being ever founded by Great Britain in the West Indies after the Parliamentary votes of 1792; much less with such blind precipitation as these rumours import; but after what we have seen lately permitted on the continent of Dutch Guyana, a subject from which for the present I

purposely

purposely abstain, nothing of this kind ought to be deemed incredible; and therefore only am I induced to implore delay, lest it should be too much to hope that right principles will permanently triumph over short-sighted avarice on this occasion.

Hitherto Sir, I earnestly request it may be observed, that my arguments have been addressed, not to the *conscience* of a British Statesman, but to his *prudence* alone; and, but that it would argue great moral insensibility in the writer, as well as do violence to right feelings, it would perhaps be wise to rest my case here; without attempting to strengthen it by what with some minds is a most dangerous support, an appeal to higher principles, than those of political expediency.

There are men who hardly scruple to avow the opinion, that in public deliberations the prohibitions of the moral law ought often to be disregarded when opposed to national advantage; and there are statesmen who have avowedly acted upon that dangerous principle in regard to the Slave Trade; holding that its abolition or continuance, was a question to be decided rather by considerations of expediency, than by the dictates of humanity and justice.

Of course it is in vain to reason with such men in public life, upon principles of mere moral obligation, whether Christian or Pagan. They will
neither

neither reprobate with St. Paul the doing evil
that good may ensue; nor hold with a Heathen
statesman " *In eadem re utilitas et turpitudo esse
non potest*" " *hoc ipsum utile putare quod turpe
sit, calamitosum est.*"* The book of entries is
their Bible; and a custom-house officer at the
bar, with an account of exports in his hand,

Plenius ac melius Chrysippo et Crantore dicit.

But unfortunately, with some who thus soar
above vulgar prejudice, the understanding does
not long profit by its enfranchisement from ordinary restraints. Having attained, what the
world perhaps is too ready to allow them, the
praise of political wisdom, they too highly prize
the peculiar source of this estimation ; and
that their exemption from the weaknesses of the
heart in public conduct may not be overlooked,
you will be sure upon any question in which
goodnatured feelings have an interest on one
side, to find their voices on the other. Hence,
these sages gradually acquire an obliquity of
vision upon every public object in which moral
considerations are involved; and their minds
are as far warped from the straight line of sound
practical judgement to the left hand, as the most
imprudent follower of abstract moral rectitude
was ever bent to the right. When a measure is
shewn to them to be wicked, it is more than half

* Cic. de offic. Lib. iii.

proved

[167]

proved to be wise. Nay their artificial taste, like other unnatural propensities, often acquires greater strength, and more powerful domination over reason and prudence, than the natural one it has supplanted could ever have attained If philanthropy has its enthusiasts, political immorality has devotees, not so ardent indeed, but more than equally blind and irrational. There are fanatics in the school of Machiavel, as well as in that of Rousseau.

I might well illustrate these remarks by reviewing some past measures relative to the Slave Trade: but besides the impropriety of such a digression, it would lead me into a subject, the discussion of which has been for the present expressly declined.

Crying mercy then of these profound politicians, and requesting them not to ruin the effect of the preceding arguments upon their own minds by reading the next following pages, I proceed to offer a brief remark or two on the *moral* character of the measure which I would persuade you to avoid.

Be not apprehensive, Sir, that I mean to lead you into any investigation of those trite and disgusting topics, the wickedness and the baseness of the slave trade.

I will not even ask you to admit, what no man who has read the evidence on the subject can conscientiously deny, that the African market

is

is supplied by criminal means alone*. But I must beg leave to recall to your recollection the votes on this subject of the Commons of Great Britain in Parliament assembled, in the year 1792.

In a Committee of the whole House, on Monday the 2d of April, in that year, upon an amended question, " *That it is the opinion of* " *this Committee that the trade carried on by* " *British subjects for the purpose of obtaining* " *slaves on the Coast of Africa ought to be gra-* " *dually abolished,*" the Committee having divided, the numbers were,

For the Question - - - - - 230
Against it - - - - - - - 85

Majority - - - - - - - - 145

In the course of the same month several subsequent debates took place, and as many questions were decided in the negative by small majorities, upon propositions for abolishing the trade at different periods *prior to* 1796.

---

* 1. *Sales of debtors, and their human pawns, or their families,* in consequence chiefly of credit given by the slave traders in brandy, tobacco, &c. with a view to such means of payment. 2. *Convictions for crimes*; mostly imputed for the sake of selling the accused and his family, such as *witchcraft*, &c. 3. *kidnapping*; and 4. *wars*; which are always proportionate in frequency and extent to the demand for captives—these, are the only sources of *vendible* or *exportable* slavery in Africa. No historical fact is better established, or less open to controversy than this.

At

At length on the 28th of April, 1792, upon an amended Question, " *That it shall not be* " *lawful to import any African negroes into any* " *British Colonies or Plantations in ships own-* " *ed or navigated by British Subjects, at any* " *time after the first day of January* 1796," it was carried in the affirmative.

Ayes - - - - - - - - - 151
Noes - - - - - - - - 132
Majority - - - - - - 19

The original Question on that day moved by Mr. Dundas, and which the minority for the most part supported, went to fix the 1st day of *January* 1800, as the period of abolition; so that though the amended resolution was carried by so small a majority as 19, it is fair to infer that the opinions were, as on the first occasion near three to one against the permanency of this commerce, and in favour of its abolition at a period now long since elapsed.

Of these resolutions the avowed principles are too well known to need explication here; and if a clear, succinct, masterly, view of the Parliamentary discussions that led to them is desired, it may be found among the Works of Mr. Gisborne*.

Those principles, Sir, were of no arbitrary or

* See Principles of Moral Philosophy, last edition, to which this tract is annexed.

mutable

mutable nature; nor such as any human legisla‑
ture can annul; they belong to the unchangea‑
ble law of God; and are of the "weightier
matters" of his law, "justice, mercy, and
truth.". The Commons of this great commer‑
cial nation in effect solemnly resolved, "*That
the slave trade was upon moral principles inde‑
fensible; and ·that it ought to be tolerated no
longer than the supposed necessities of the West
India Colonies, possessed by Great Britain in
1792, indispensibly required.*" Different opinions
prevailed as to the proper extent of the term
during which it should be suffered to continue;
but except in the small minority of 85, out of
315 votes, not a voice was found to defend the
trade on any other ground but that of existing
necessity. Even those members of that small
minority who gave their reasons, for the
most part equally relied upon this defence,
though they would not concur in then fixing a
time for future abolition. The condemnation
of this traffic therefore as a voluntary branch of
commerce, was not merely the act of a majority,
composed of rigid rectitudinarians. Most of
the advocates for state convenience, and the
champions of Liverpool, concurred in it. It was
the declared sense of Mr. Dundas—if I mis‑
take not Sir it was your own—Nay, were I to se‑
lect from the debates on the slave trade, the
                                        most

most striking passages of strong and unqualified reprobation of that commerce upon moral principles, I should perhaps cull them from the speeches of Mr. Dundas, and of the supporters of that middle ground which he, fatally for Africa, maintained.

The principles thus asserted by the Commons of Great Britain have never been retracted; on the contrary a Bill grounded upon them was sent up to the Lords so recently as 1799.

Mean time, the echo of the loud clamours of the national conscience of this commercial country, were heard in other nations; and produced the very reformation in their trade, which the commons stood so solemnly pledged for in our own. The states of America passed acts of immediate abolition; and Denmark issued an ordinance to terminate her commerce on the slave coast at an early period. As to France, and the states dependent on her, the extinction of their slave trade was less perhaps the result of principle than necessity; but in fact, not a negro was transported from Africa after the commencement of the war under the flag of the Republic, nor a slave imported into her remaining West India possessions. When British Guineamen were captured by her cruizers in the West Indies, a case very frequent, the Africans were not allowed to be sold for the benefit of the captors;

but

but immediately enfranchised on arrival at her Colonial Ports*.

An argument much relied on by one of your present colleagues, a zealous defender of this commerce, was thus done away; and in its stead a new tie of an honorary nature bound the Commons to consistency. Nor is it material to say that the Republic or other European nations have revived or propose to revive this trade, while they have so much reason to conclude that Great Britain will not concur in renouncing it; unless it can be shewn that we have treated with them for a general compact to make the sacrifice universal. If any diplomatic proposition of that nature was made to France, for the credit of this country, let the fact be made public; but if not, the relapse of the French or other nations into this iniquity, will be no excuse for our own apostacy; of which it will be rather an effect, than a motive, and an aggravation, rather than an excuse. Supposing however that other nations had not been deceived by, or acted upon our resolutions,

---

* The most satisfactory evidence of this fact has been found in the papers of neutral vessels from the French Colonies taken as prizes and prosecuted in our Admiralty Courts. *See the cases of the Active and Adeline before the Lords Commissioners of Appeals in Prize Causes in* 1802. *Further evidence on the part of the Captors, page* 45. The same fact has also clearly appeared in other Appeals.

they

they are still binding in honor as well as conscience upon the British Commons, and are still the uncancelled records of our self-conviction if wantonly in principle transgressed.

Under such circumstances what name ought to be given to the project of those who would found a new Slave Colony at Trinidada? Instead of binding up the bleeding veins of Africa in 1796, they would in the second year of the 19th century, enlarge her wounds by new and more fatal incisions. Instead of merely sustaining those houses built by blood and misery which we then owned, they would mark out the foundations of a new and enormous edifice, to be raised, and kept in repair for ages to come, by the same horrible materials. They would open a new West Indies, and prepare new fleets of slave-ships to drain the yet remaining blood of Africa, and stimulate her wretched children to new crimes, that our new shambles may be filled.

The utmost period to which even Mr. Dundas would have protracted the miseries of that hapless continent, has arrived; nay, the sun has twice run his annual round, since Mr. Pitt, with the full concurrence of that too powerful friend, was to see the benign light of civilization begin to shed on the
dark

dark horizon of Africa at least an evening ray—

* " Illic sera rubens accendit lumina vesper!"

Alas! how unreal have proved the prospects so eloquently painted! In that gloomy region not a star has yet risen, but it is profound and hopeless darkness still.

————intempesta silet nox
Semper, et obtentâ densantur nocte tenebræ.

To recede from a generous purpose of reformation, is however far less reproachful to a great nation, than to enter upon new crimes of which she has felt and admitted the turpitude; and when the bounds of acknowledged and repented transgression are willingly enlarged beyond those limits which bad habit has made it difficult to contract, it argues more than a want of virtuous energy; it indicates a character rotten to the core, and in which the influence of moral sensibility is wholly subverted.

And shall a great nation like this, Sir, expose itself to such foul reproach! Shall Great Britain, after avowing the smart of an awakened conscience, and promising like a poor Mag-

* See Mr. Pitt's incomparable speech in the debate of April 2d, 1792.

dalen

dalen to reform when relieved from the ab-
horrid necessity of sinning, relapse into
deeper prostitution the moment a new settlement is offered!! Forbid it that sentiment
to which may Englishmen never become in-
sensible! forbid it the sense of national dignity
and virtue!

For apostacy so infamous as such conduct
would amount to, well might Englishmen blush;
for let it be remembered that it was not merely
by the votes of the Commons that the Slave
Trade was condemned: a vast majority of the
nation at large anticipated by their declared
opinions and their wishes, that solemn and
righteous judgment: and by whom has the self-
condemning sentence been reversed? The Lords
indeed have not given their concurrence; but
even they have pronounced no different verdict
on the evidence, upon which the solemn cause
is still depending before them. If that House
of Parliament has not echoed, at least it has not
expressly negatived, the conclusions of the
Commons, and the petitions of the people.

Is there then to be found in history a precedent for national inconsistency so very base
as the opening a new Slave Colony by the
African trade would at this juncture amount
to? Nations indeed have sometimes acted in-
congruously enough with their professions and
avowed principles; but it has generally, or always,

ways, been in the pursuit of objects, which
whether real or ostensible, were in their kind less
sordid than the bribe now held out in Trinidada by the Slave trade; from motives something
less grovelling than mere avarice; and rarely, if
ever, at the expence of principles so very sacred
as those we are now called on to sacrifice or to
maintain. The crime would I conceive be quite
unparallelled in enormity; and there is hardly
a civilized nation on earth that might not afterwards look down upon this favoured land,
boastful of its public virtue, and apply to us
with some little variation the reproof of one of
our own poets for a vice of a different character:

" O Britain infamous for *avarice*,
" An island in thy morals more depraved,
" Than the whole world of rationals beside;
" In ambient waves plunge thy polluted head,
" Wash the dire stain, nor fhock the Continent."

Perhaps even with those Latitudinarians, who
disclaim in public life the obligations of morality, national character at least, may be held
of some importance; and they may feel that
the credit of the country, demands some little attention to consistency on this occasion.
Let me suggest to them therefore, that if the
Slave Trade is to be thus extended, the votes
of 1792 ought to be reversed; and erased
like the resolutions on the Middlesex election
from

from the Journals of the House. I would also recommend that the great body of evidence respecting the nature and sources of the African trade which was laid at that æra before Parliament, and so strongly impressed the conscience of the Commons, may be committed to the flames; unless upon a second inspection it should be found like some cabalistic inscriptions mentioned in the Arabian Tales, to have since changed its form and signification, But for such of the great speakers in favour of abolition, whether immediate or gradual, as may now countenance such an extension of the Slave Trade or allow it to pass without their sincere opposition, a more difficult labour will remain. They must collect and destroy every impression of those powerful speeches, the eloquence of which has given them a wide diffusion in the libraries of the present day, and would embalm them for posterity; lest they should hereafter hold a lamp to the hearts of their authors, when the anxious politics of the present day shall be too remote in time and interest to surround with false rays the great public actors engaged in them, while the eternal principles of morals shall remain, to measure by an unchanging scale, the true magnitude or littleness of character.

But I am wronging those great men of both parties who have supported the cause of aboli-

N   tion,

tion, by supposing for a moment that they could fall into such reproachful apostacy. That they would if necessary vindicate the honour of illustrious talents by a far different conduct, and would be supported not only by the voice of Parliament, but of the nation at large, is I trust unquestionable. I would hope however that there will be found as well within the Cabinet, as without, a perfect unanimity of opinion against a wanton and enormous enlargement of the Trade for the purpose in question, whatever differences may still subsist as to its immediate abolition.

***

If the reasons which have been offered against the colonization of Trinidada in the accustomed West India mode, are not all inconclusive; if moral principles solemnly and repeatedly recognized by one branch of the Legislature, and not disclaimed by the other, ought not to be needlessly and grossly violated; or if all the serious prudential objections to that iniquitous project which have been here urged, are not too weak to forbid at least its immediate adoption ; my argument imposes on me no necessity to go further, and to point out positive advantages that may be derived from this

this new Colony by an opposite mode of treatment.

There are however great and extensive be-
nefits, of an innocent and unobjectionable kind,
which the nation may reap from this cession;
and I regret that the necessity of drawing to a
conclusion prevents my now speaking of them
so fully and distinctly as they deserve.

Of the *commercial* capacities of the Island
something was lately said in Parliament, and their
value was not exaggerated.

That the deep and capacious Bay of Paria,
effectually guarded as it is by its well enclosed
situation, if not also by its geographical place,
from the peril of hurricanes,* will soon be
the favourite resort of West India commerce,
hardly admits of a doubt; and already experience has begun in some degree to prove, that it
will become a most useful and important *entre-
pôt*, between the manufacturers of Great Britain, and the traders of Spanish America.

To Trinidada, the Spaniards already resort with
their dollars and rich native commodities, in
order to purchase the cottons of Manches-
ter, and other manufactures of this country,
so much in demand in their own. For these,
they have been long accustomed to frequent
with their small vessels the ports of the British

* Hurricanes have never yet been known so far to the
southward.

Islands,

Islands, at a great distance from their own coasts, though admitted only by connivance, contrary to our Acts of Parliament, as well as to the laws of Spain. But they have visited not British ports only: those of all other European nations who possessed any Settlement in the Charribbean seas, have partaken of the benefit ; and foreign manufactures have consequently in some degree supplanted our own.

In these commercial voyages, much was naturally added by the length of the passage to the degree of a danger most formidable in its kind ; perpetual imprisonment, and hard labour, as well as confiscation of property, being the penalties incurred under their own laws, by these adventurers when seized in the course of that illicit traffic: and this risque during the passage naturally diminished an intercourse, which it could not wholly suppress. Our own merchants tempted by the enormous profits they obtained, were sometimes bold enough to embark in this trade and to supply the craving markets of the Spanish settlements in British vessels, at the peril of the same fearful consequences attendant on detection and capture. The laxity of fiscal police in the interior of these settlements is so great, or the connivance of revenue officers there, from a sense of public necessity, so universal, that the danger incurred by the Spanish smugglers seems to be confined to the transport of the commodities

modities *by sea ;* and therefore when that danger shall be materially abridged by the proximity of the foreign port with which they trade, the commerce will probably soon and greatly increase.

It is still more probable that almost all the scattered streams of this lucrative trade which have heretofore flowed from different points of the Spanish continent in the vicinity of Trinidada, to the English, French, Dutch, and Danish Charribbee Islands, will be collected together by a channel so inviting as that which will now present itself in the Gulph of Paria, at only three miles distance from the main.

I would not be understood as meaning to recommend a species of commerce, interdicted by the laws of the two countries between the subjects of which it obtains. Whether wants the most urgent, and a necessity which is no less than that of being clothed when naked, may excuse the Spanish colonists in breaking through the jealous and tyrannical restrictions of a royal ordinance, and whether also the British merchant is absolved from the duty of obeying an Act of Parliament when the officers of the Customs are officially instructed to dispense with it, * are questions which I am not bound to discuss. I

* It is by instructions from the Board of Customs, that the British Ports in the West Indies are open to this trade, contrary to the Acts of Navigation.

speak

speak of what commerce may be expected at Trinidada, not of what ought to be allowed.

Let me however digress so far, as to suggest that it would be honourable to your administration to remove, if possible, these stumbling blocks out of the way of commercial morals; and that the cession of Trinidada may perhaps furnish a fair opportunity of effecting it. Spain, conscious of her inability to prevent by any laws an intercourse to which there are on both sides so great temptations, and to which our possession of the Gulph of Paria will now give new facilities; may perhaps be disposed to purchase by a regulated permission of the trade, some conventional security against the evils of contraband dealings, and against other inconveniencies which she may apprehend in a political view, from our near approach to her continental possessions. As to the British laws which prohibit this commerce, their repeal has as I apprehend been prevented only by the fear of giving offence to the Court of Madrid. It would certainly be indecent openly to legalize a trade with the subjects of any power contrary to its own prohibitions.

Though the illicit and clandestine nature of this commerce would certainly contribute to the peculiar attractions of Trinidada, this port would have claims enough to secure to it also a decided preference, in the event of a more general

neral intercourse with the continent being legalized by the government of Spain.

But our new colony has other commercial advantages of a novel and peculiar kind. If by vicinity to Laguayra, and the other ports of the province of Caraccas, it invites the commerce of the Spanish Colonies on the Main, it offers the same motive of preference to the colonists of Demerara, Berbice, Issequibo, and Surinam, which are all at a short distance to the *windward*, on the same rich continent.

Of these settlements, restored by the late treaty to the Dutch Republic, the two former, if the national character of the chief inhabitants and proprietors were to constitute that of the soil, might be called British Colonies. By adventurers from the English Islands many of their finest plantations were owned before the war; and such extensive tracts of their uncleared lands have been purchased and settled by our fellow-subjects since the capture of those colonies, that the Dutch planters are probably inferior both in number and fortune to the British.

What restrictions the policy of the European masters may impose on their reviving trade, it is not easy to foresee: but the want of capital and credit will in all probability lead to an indulgent system; and of whatever commercial intercourse they may allow to foreigners, their enterprising British neighbours will be the first to

reap

reap the benefit. Habit will conspire with more rational grounds of preference, to recommend the manufactures of this country; and unless very strange reverses take place, the British market, when the certainty and convenience of its returns are taken into account, will probably be long the most eligible destination for the consignment of West India products. This double inducement, under a government professing to be popular, will either bend the law to the general convenience, or make the general convenience too strong for the law; and in either event, Trinidada may be expected to become a warehouse for the supply of these flourishing settlements with the merchandize of Europe; and for the reception of their produce in return.

Hither also, the exports from the United States of America ultimately destined for the supply of the colonies on the Main, will naturally find their way; especially during the hurricane season, or when from the crops being over, or from a temporary glut of such commodities, immediate returns are not to be expected from the place of final destination. Here, as in a secure and convenient magazine, those essential supplies will be deposited, as of late years they were for the use of our own Islands at St. Eustatius; and the merchant of Trinidada will either receive a middle profit, or a factor's commission,

sion, from the exporter of North America on the one hand, and the planter of Guyana on the other.

From these considerations, which might be much further extended, this settlement will probably become an emporium of Western commerce, superior to any that has yet been seen between the tropics.

So far, Sir, are these great commercial views from recommending, that they evidently and strongly tend to interdict, the further introduction of slavery, and the Slave Trade, into Trinidada.

The footing which the baneful West India system has already gained there is insignificantly small, when compared to the extent of the Island; and if its further progress shall be prevented, you may gradually fix in that new soil a firm and tranquil dominion, so as to perpetuate these great commercial advantages; instead of possessing them by that precarious, uneasy, and costly tenure, by which the sovereignty of a slave colony in the West Indies must always in future be held. Let therefore the great and innocent value of this important cession, be a new argument against applying it to the guilty uses that short sighted avarice would suggest.

Are then, it may be asked, the fertile lands of this extensive Island to remain in the same unproductive state in which Spanish indolence

has

has left them? Better so, than that they should
be watered by human blood, and the tears of
human wretchedness. But happily, this is not
the only alternative.

No Sir, a beneficent Providence, has put into
your hands, an inestimable treasury, of more than
commercial, or than agricultural wealth; comprising these indeed, to a large extent, but containing a pearl of far higher price, to arrest the
improvident alienation of which, is no unimportant object of this Address.

You have in this great acquisition, the means
of most favourably trying an experiment of
unspeakable importance to mankind; an experiment never tried before; and of which the success might in future produce such extensive good,
as to indemnify humanity for all the evils of the
late dreadful war: Africa might hereafter be delivered by it from the devastation of the Slave
Trade; and a new system founded in the West
Indies, gradually, but surely corrective, of all the
evils of the old.

To hold at least a highly probable chance,
of such great effects, and of attaining with
them, a yet unknown degree of colonial strength
and prosperity, you have scarcely a sacrifice to
make; nor to call upon the country for a single
active effort. Almost all that will be necessary,
is, to abstain, from what I hope has upon other
views, been proved to be a most impolitic, and
ill-timed

ill-timed alienation of the public domains in
Trinidada; and to prohibit the importation of
slaves, or at least of negroes to remain in bondage, for the further settlement of that Island.

If, to purchase a chance of such gigantic
good, a large price were to be paid by the public, I will not wrong the feelings of Englishmen
so much, as to doubt that they would chearfully
ratify the contract   But, if there be justice
in the preceding arguments, the plan I propose
to you, is one pregnant with the only means of
future œconomy, and abiding wealth, in the
West Indies; and therefore it would be erro-
neous to consider as any pecuniary sacrifice,
the means I have next to suggest: more especially, as they will only keep pace with the success of the experiment.

In addition then, to a provident reservation
of the crown lands, and the prohibition of im-
porting slaves for their future culture, *Let a
portion of that rich and unopened soil, be sold at
a low price, or granted freely, to all who will undertake, as the condition of the tenure, and on
peril of reverter to the crown, to settle and cul-
tivate it by the labor of* FREE NEGROES.

As further encouragement, it will be necessary that whoever shall add by importation to
the common stock of free cultivators, shall have
secured to him a pre-emption of their labor for a
reasonable time, upon terms to be regulated by
law;

law; or in other words, that they shall for a term of years be placed in the known relation of indented servants, to the planter for the culture of whose estate, and at whose expence, they shall be brought to the Island and enfranchised.

That the nature of this new condition may be unequivocally distinguished from the state, inadequately defined by the term " slavery," and may not degenerate into that pernicious bondage, its limits must be clearly and anxiously fixed by positive law, and guarded by the most vigorous sanctions. The fundamental properties of negro slavery, to which in my first Letter I called your attention, must be wholly reversed. The qualified and temporary property of the master in the labor of his imported servants, must not be transferable at his discretion : still less must it be liable to be severed, unless under very special circumstances, from the tenure of the land. The wages to be given, whether in money or food, must be determined by law ; and so must the general maximum of work to be exacted. Above all, the brutalizing method of enforcing labor by the immediate application or terror of the driver's lash, must be totally prohibited. That shameful peculiarity of negro bondage, that bane of moral character in the slave, is utterly inconsistent with the happy formation of a new system, as well as with the effectual reformation of the old.

Some

Some power of correction for obstinate idleness or bad conduct, it may be necessary to intrust to the master; but its exercise must be jealously superintended by the law, and its abuse severely punished; forfeiture of the right of service ought to be one consequence of any serious ill treatment of a servant.

To enforce such laws, magistrates of great respectability, independent of the community in which they live, and precluded from holding landed property in the Island, ought to be appointed, and armed with extraordinary powers; and their personal security in the exercise of their offices ought to be anxiously provided for. They should be made amenable for official misconduct to British Tribunals only; and should be obliged to record the evidence on which they proceed, in order to secure and facilitate the due investigation of their judgments, upon appeals to a higher tribunal in this country; which appeals ought in all important cases to be allowed, and under such regulations as will prevent expence and delay to the parties as much as possible, and at the same time check a litigious spirit.

But the grand and essential spring, and guard of all, is *Parliamentary Legislation*.

I would earnestly advise you, Sir, in the forming a Constitution for this new Colony, to avoid the fatal error of giving to it, in its infancy, a Legislative Assembly. At least until its
population

population and wealth become such as to promise a respectable representation, let the power of making laws for its internal government, rest exclusively with Parliament.

Something has in a former part of this Letter been said of the inconveniences that have arisen from the institution of petty Legislative Assemblies, which represent and sit in the centre of the small communities over which they preside, and of their inaptitude to correct such local evils even, as seem to fall within their most peculiar province. The remarks there made, may be extended beyond the consideration of the slave laws; and, I know not, the mischiefs springing from those laws excepted, a source of greater political evils in our small West India Islands, than their having been separately complimented with a pigmy model of the British Constitution. That noble machine, believe me, does not work well upon so small a scale. It is however sufficiently evident, that in the first rude stage of colonization, the settlers must be peculiarly unfit to form such an Assembly, as may be safely intrusted with the momentous business of forming or improving a municipal code; especially a code, to be built upon principles so opposite to the former habits and notions of West Indians, as those which I trust will be the basis of the laws of Trinidada.

To these practical hints, brief and general as
they

they are, I am aware that many objections will occur. Of those that seem the most important I have well considered the force; and regret that it is impossible, without delaying this publication too long, and extending its bulk beyond all reasonable bounds, to state them distinctly, with the satisfactory answers, by which I think they might be repelled.

The difficulty that in my estimate has the greatest weight, is one which the West India party would probably not choose to bring forward. It arises from a fact of which from familiar acquaintance with some of our old Colonies, I have a clear conviction, *that such cheapness of labour is by no means to be expected from the voluntary industry, however great, of negroes in a state of freedom, as now excites the enterprize, and splendidly rewards the success of the planter, in places where slavery is established.* I admit therefore that Trinidada would not on the plan proposed hold out to adventurers so good a field for the acquisition of a rapid fortune, as our slave colonies, while we are able to preserve them, may in general afford. And as a consequence of this concession, I must further explicitly declare my opinion to be, that if blind avarice is to be gratified by the most lucrative sale of the vacant lands that can be effected, the purchaser must be indulged with the cheap accustomed mode of cultivation. But if the

more

more liberal policy here recommended, should be
adopted in the disposal of those fertile lands, speculation I doubt not will be sufficiently active to
make the setttlement soon very populous and
flourishing ; notwithstanding the enhanced price
of labour, and all other objections that can be
stated.

The planter's gains, though not so great,
as where slave labor on a successful estate is
attainable, would be more uniform, and infinitely
more secure ; while the abundance of land
with which he might be furnished for raising
provisions, the richness of the soil, the peculiar
practicability of employing the plough in the
large savannas of level land with which the
Island abounds, and other means by which human labour when no longer cheapened by the
effects of slavery, would be carefully saved,
would all tend to lessen the force of this chief
objection, and to invite settlement under the
new system at Trinidada.

This consideration would if the planter could
be sufficiently encouraged, become a great
recommendation of the plan proposed, rather than an objection to it. If the negro
were better paid, or better maintained in return for his labor, to whom would the profit
ultimately result, but to the manufacturers,
merchants, and ship-owners of Great Britain ;
and through them to the revenu and maritime
resources

resources of the Empire? This, Sir, is a wide
and interesting topic from which I am sorry to
abstain. I must however avoid digression; and
therefore will only so far explain the hint as to
observe, that three thousand free negro labourers
would probably purchase more European commodities and manufactures imported in British
shipping, than are now consumed by ten thousand
slaves. Your West India ships now on an average
carry out to the Islands in actual freight not
more than one third of their tonnage; but the
ships trading to Trinidada, would probably be as
fully laden on their outward, as on their home-
ward, voyage.

Of other apparent objections to this interesting plan I must for the present wholly avoid the
discussion; as well as of a most important and
delicate question, "*Whether slavery being first
effectually prohibited in Trinidada, importation
from Africa might justifiably be permitted, to
those who should chuse to enfranchise the negroes
they might import, with a view to the more speedy
and effectual settlement of the Island?*" It is
not merely from the necessity of hastening to a
conclusion, but from the difficulty of this question in a moral view, that I decline the discussion
of it under the present unsettled circumstances
of the case.

When it shall be expressly and firmly decided
not to tolerate a new Colony of Slaves, it will be
time enough to consider, whether the African trade

o   may

may conscienciously be made to minister to a new and beneficent system, which is to operate its own extinction; and provide like the viper out of its own substance the means of healing more speedily the wounds it has inflicted. Let me not however be misunderstood. Of the duty of totally and immediately abolishing the Slave Trade I am far indeed from entertaining a doubt; and have adverted to the question of allowing it to feed a free and happy population at Trinidada, only under the apprehension that Parliament may still allow it to widen the circle of the deplorable bondage subsisting in our other Islands.

In that case only, I find it difficult to say that to import a hundred negroes upon the terms of manumission, immediately from Africa, would be more culpable than to bring them circuitously through Barbadoes or Grenada. To remove Creole slaves upon such terms from the old Islands, and supply their place with Africans, would clearly be an ill judged preference. It would be to enfranchise those who from the corrupting habits of bondage are the least fit for freedom; and to subject those to the yoke, upon whom its pressure would from novelty be the most intolerable. Nor would freedom to the Creole negro, though an inestimable boon, be unalloyed with pain, when to receive it he must be banished perhaps from all his beloved connections; a mi-

sery

sery which the poor African must equally sustain to whatever part of the West Indies he may be carried: in this respect therefore, the supposed substitution would be a needless duplication of wretchedness.

Though it is not without pain that I offer advice upon a condition, the very idea of which is so dishonourable to my country, as the prolongation of the Slave Trade, I feel it a duty to add that supposing that case to exist, another important consideration may arise in favour of negro liberty in our new Colony.

Were freedom established in that island, and African negroes allowed to be imported for the more speedy encrease of its population, considerable numbers of them ought in my judgment to be purchased by government, enrolled into regiments, disciplined, and maintained as a permanent garrison, at Trinidada. This expedient, which has already been applied on a small scale to the defence of our Islands, has hitherto been found highly advantageous, and productive of no bad effects; and though the augmentation of this new species of soldiery may, as before admitted, be liable to some prudential objections in places where slavery obtains, it could in a free Colony give no just occasion for jealousy or apprehension.

Such troops, peculiarly fitted as they would be by the same bodily qualities that recommended them

to

to the slave merchant, and by their yet un-
broken spirit, for military duties, knowing no
European tongue but our own, strongly attached to the government which redeemed them
from captivity, and connected with the community around them by no sympathies but such
as would serve to fortify that disposition, would
be excellent defenders against the hostile attempts of France; and not Trinidada alone, but
our other Islands, might find in them if numerous enough, the best attainable means of
security against the new perils that are so evidently approaching.

This Island, which lies to the windward of
almost all our other West India possessions,
would be a most convenient station from whence
to send reinforcements to them on any emergency; and from the same cause, let me inci-
dentally observe, the new system supposed to be
established at Trinidada, would be the more in-
offensive to its Sister Colonies; because that
windward position would render it very difficult for the slaves of our other Islands to make
their escape into that land of freedom, supposing even its own interior police not sufficiently well regulated to prevent such abuses.

Beyond the very valuable regular force, that
might thus without occasion of disquietude be
maintained, it would be adviseable to form the
male negroes of a proper age into a militia, as

is

is now the practice in regard to all the free inhabitants of our Colonies. By such means this
valuable Island would, when its settlement should
be a little advanced, become perfectly invulner-
able ; and its defence would nearly cease to be
a burthen on the finances, while it would in no
degree drain the population of the mother
country.

Of the fidelity of the armed negroes there
could in this case be no reasonable doubt; for
the cause of Great Britain would be their own.
Instead therefore of lying at the mercy of the
French Republic in any future war, this powerful Colony might perhaps enable us to overawe
all the valuable settlements of France, Spain,
and Holland, on the neighbouring Continent ;
while the example of its strength and prosperity,
might gradually attract imitation in the old
Islands, deliver us from the guilt of the Slave
Trade, and perpetuate to us in the West Indies,
an innocent, safe, and flourishing dominion.

Great then Sir, beyond any former precedent, is the colonial crisis to which I have endeavoured to attract your attention.

While a war of unparalleled importance has
been agitating the bosom of Europe, and over-
turning her ancient establishments ; a new order

der of things has arisen in the West, pregnant
probably with new wars, and with new civil revolutions in that quarter of the globe.

That sword which has spread desolation over
the old world, is now drawn against the inhabitants of the new. The same Republic which
under pretence of giving liberty, has subjugated
and enslaved some of the happiest of European
nations, is now under pretences equally false,
attempting to reimpose on her enfranchised negroes the yoke of domestic bondage; the only
yoke which after all her vaunts she has even by
accident broken, and compared to the weight of
which, her own military despotism may without
irony or grimace, be called by the name of freedom.

Nor is it only to the negroes of St. Domingo,
who revolted from the cart-whip, and owe her
only a constrained recognition of their enfranchisement, that France would re-apply the
coercion of the drivers. From the black colonists of her windward settlements, this consistent and grateful Republic would recall the
gift of freedom which by her own laws she
invited them to accept, and which they have
faithfully and bravely repaid. Regardless of the
important services they rendered her at the most
arduous crisis of her affairs, and of eight years
undeviating fidelity, she has forced by Lacrosse's attempts the negroes of Guadaloupe
into

into insurrection; and if the assertions of her government deserve credit, has restored the Slave Trade at Cayenne.

Such is Gallic attachment to the principles of freedom and justice!!

But to these counter-revolutionary views, firm resistance has already been opposed. Guadaloupe is already in the undisputed possession of the negroes; and Buonaparte, in his more than Syrian enterprise against St. Domingo, seems likely to be encountered by difficulties not less insuperable than the walls of Acre.

Of the probable consequences of this important though distant war, I have attempted a fair investigation; and whatever may be their nature in regard to France, they have appeared to be in every possible result big with early perils to the Colonial interests of Great Britain. Even in that event which might be least incompatible with the safety of private property in our Colonies, their political relation to this country will be imminently endangered. The attainment of the apparent objects of the Republic has been shewn to be what we are bound no less in a national view to deprecate, than the freedom and independency of the negroes.

Such being our prospects, I have proceeded to enquire what measures those who preside over the affairs of this great Empire ought to pursue in this alarming crisis, and what to avoid;
and

and though the practical conclusions which have been suggested are chiefly of a negative kind, it has been attempted to point out some measures of active preparation, by which the approaching perils may be lessened, and our great maritime and commercial interests in the West Indies, enabled finally perhaps to ride out the storm.

On the objections which may be expected to be raised to these remedial expedients I have not been silent. The most obvious have been noticed and repelled. But if through the delicacy of the case, the novelty and difficulty of the measures proposed, or the formidable opposition made by parties whose particular interests are involved, you should be induced rather to await the natural issue of the disease than resort to such troublesome means of relief, at least the impolicy of urging forward the dangerous crisis, has I trust been sufficiently proved.

Were the justice and dignity of the nation not irreconcileably opposed to the monstrous project which some minds have not been ashamed to conceive;—were the feelings of Englishmen prepared for an alliance with the French Republic, in a war like that in which she has embarked at St. Domingo;—were we willing to imbue our hands in the blood of men who *if they had no conventional claims on our neutrality*, have yet given us no offence, and possess

the

the negative merit of having abstained during
critical times from hostilities against us ;—were
we mean enough to become scavengers to the
Great Nation, by helping her to scour her Colonies from what she now chooses to consider as
the filth of her own revolutions ;* I say Sir,
were British minds ripe for all this deep humiliation, it has I trust been demonstrated that
they ought in plain policy to be saved from it ;
and that the fatuity of assisting France in this
new war would be such as could only be sur-
passed by its baseness.

It has been attempted further to shew that
if neither through the means I have suggested, nor any others that can be devised, our
slave-peopled Colonies can be so strengthened
as to be secured from the new dangers of their

* The most *modest* State Paper perhaps that has issued
from the Government press of France, even in these days of
persiflage and hypocrisy, is General *Le Clerc*'s late Proclamation
to the Negroes of St Domingo, wherein he gravely declaims
against those " *abstract principles* " that he supposes to have
banished the cart-whip; and invites the Negroes to partake
the freedom which France as he says " *has extended to all
the Countries in Europe that she has conquered—therefore
cannot be supposed capable of withholding from* them."—
The pattern to be sure is in European eyes not very inviting;
and yet like the gloomy finery of the undertakers' journeymen,
this French freedom would be far too costly for the poor negroes long to wear, should they listen to the worthy General.
—They would soon be called upon to strip, and put on their
former rags.

situation,

situation, at least we ought not at the present
alarming conjuncture needlessly to encrease their
extent, and to enlarge the too great proportion
of our commercial capital already dependent on
their fate. If the foundation be incurably bad,
let us not add another story to the building ; nor
deposit in it more of our most costly effects.
The fall of our Slave Colonies is probable
enough, and would be fatal enough, without adding Trinidada, settled by large and recent mer-
cantile speculations, to their number.

Let us rather try to found in that extensive
Island a new and happy system of colonization,
which while it produces wealth, may with an
equal progress furnish free, strong and faithful
hands to defend it. Let the critical state of our
Western Empire teach us the right use of this, its
important augmentation ; and lead us so to settle
our new Island, that Trinidada may become at
once an example, and a protection ; a farm of
experiment, and a fortress ; to the rest of our
Sugar Colonies.

In offering you a chart whereby to steer
through the dangerous straits we have entered,
the course of greatest safety has been found happily to coincide with that of moral rectitude and
honor ; and to be, as far as relates to Trinidada,
the only course which we can pursue without
shipwreck of consistency, as well as of conscien-
tious principle.

From

From these higher considerations I could not wholly abstain; but independently of these, the basis of public expediency sufficiently supports the practical opinions that have been offered. By the coolest prudential views I am content that those opinions should be tried; but let prejudice on the other hand concede, that sound policy is not always at variance with the principles of moral obligation; that measures may be very unwise although they are flagitiously wicked; and that there are cases in which a Statesman may by adhering to the dictates of humanity and justice most effectually promote the true interests of his country.

I am, Sir, &c. &c.

APPENDIX.

APPENDIX.

N° I.

LIBERTY AND EQUALITY.

Extract of the Decree of the National Conven-
tion of the 25th Pluviose, the 2d year of the
French Republic, One and Indivisible.

" THE National Convention declares that
" Negro Slavery in all the Colonies is abolished;
" and consequently that all men without dis-
" tinction of colour domiciled in the Colonies
" are French Citizens, and intitled to all the
" rights confirmed by the Constitution. It
" looks to the Committee of Public Safety con-
" stantly to report on the measures to be taken
" to secure the execution of the present decree.

" Examined by the Inspectors, &c.

" Signed, &c. &c.

To the above extract was subjoined the following Proclamation, by the Commissaries who
attended the expedition to Point-à-Pitre.

" CITIZENS!

" Citizens !

"A Republican Government is not supported by chains, nor slavery! The National Convention, therefore, has proceeded solemnly to decree liberty to the negroes ; and to intrust the mode of putting the law in force to the Commissaries whom they have delegated in the Colonies. It is necessary then to attend to the natural emancipation, and civil organization of this body. First, To a proper equality ; without which the political machine is like a clock whose pendulum has lost its equilibrium and perpetual action. Secondly, an administration general and particular, which shall guarantee property already accumulated, and the produce of labour and industry.

"Citizens of all colours! your happiness depends upon this law, and its execution. The delegates of the nation guarantee to you a system which will be the safeguard of all the friends of the French Republic, against those who have already oppressed, and wish again to oppress them. But it is necessary that the white Citizens shall give cordially and fraternally a competent salary for the work of their black, and other brethren of colour; and it is also necessary, that the latter should learn and never forget, that those who have no property are obliged to labour for their own subsistence, and that

of

of their families ; and contribute with the rest
by this mean, to the support of their Country.

" Citizens, you are not to become equal but to
enjoy happiness, and let all partake of it. He
that is an oppressor of his fellow Citizens is a
monster, that ought to be immediately banished
from human society ! The Delegates of the
Nation order all administrative bodies, municipalities, armed forces, and all individuals to put
into execution the law proclaimed at the head
of these presents without delay; and they depend upon the loyalty of all individuals for the
safety of the French Republic, and put under
the protection of the law all Citizens, their
property and the produce of their industry and
labour whatever it may be.

" They order the seal to be affixed to the publication of the present law and proclamation; at
Point-à-Pitre in the Island of Guadaloupe the
19th Prairial, 2d year of the French Republic,
One and Indivisible.

(Signed.)   Pierre Chretienne.
Victor Hugues."

APPENDIX.

APPENDIX.

N° II.

Toussaint L'Ouverture, General in Chief of the Army of St. Domingo, to all the Civil and Military Officers of the Island.

CITIZENS,

AFTER putting an end to the War in the South, our first duty has been to return thanks to the Almighty, which we have done with a zeal becoming so great a blessing. Now, Citizens, it is necessary to consecrate all our moments to the prosperity of St. Domingo, to the public tranquillity, and consequently to the welfare of our Fellow-citizens.

But to attain this end in an effectual manner, all the Civil and Military Officers must make it their business, every one in their respective departments, to perform the duties of their offices with devotion and attachment to the public welfare.

You

You will easily conceive, Citizens, that agriculture is the support of Government; since it is the foundation of commerce and wealth, the source of arts and industry, it keeps every body employed, as being the mechanism of all trades: and from the moment that every individual becomes useful, it creates public tranquillity; disturbances disappear, together with idleness, by which they are commonly generated, and every one peaceably enjoys the fruits of his industry.

Officers, civil and military, this is what you must aim at; such is the plan to be adopted, which I prescribe to you; and I declare, in the most peremptory manner, that it shall be enforced. My country demands this salutary step; I am bound to it by my office, and the security of our liberties demands it imperiously.

But in order to secure our liberties, which are indispensible to our happiness, every individual must be usefully employed, so as to contribute to the public good, and the general tranquillity.

Considering that the soldier, who has sacred duties to perform, as being the safeguard of the people, and in perpetual activity, to execute the orders of his Chief, either for maintaining interior tranquillity, or for fighting abroad the enemies of the country, is strictly subordinate to his superior officers; and as it is of great importance

portance that overseers, drivers, and field-negroes, who in like manner have their superiors,
should conduct themselves as officers, subalterns, and soldiers, in whatever may concern
them.

Considering that, when an officer, a subaltern,
or a soldier, deviates from his duty, he is delivered over to a Court-martial, to be tried and
punished according to the laws of the Republic,
for in military service no rank is to be favoured
when guilty ; the overseers, drivers, and field-
negroes, as subject to constant labour, and
equally subordinate to their superiors, shall be
punished in like manner, in case of failure in
their respective duties.

Whereas a soldier cannot leave his company,
his battalion, or half-brigade, and enter into
another, without the severest punishment, unless provided with a permission in due form
from his Chief; field-negroes are forbidden to quit
their respective plantations without a lawful permission : this is by no means attended to, since
they change their place of labour as they please,
go to and fro, and pay not the least attention to
agriculture, though the only means of furnish-
ing sustenance to the military, their protectors :
they even conceal themselves in towns, in villages, and mountains, where, allured by the
enemies of good order, they live by plunder,
and in a state of open hostility to society.

P

Whereas,

Whereas, since the revolution, labourers of both sexes, then too young to be employed in the field, refuse to go to it now under pretext of freedom, spend their time in wandering about, and give a bad example to the other cultivators; while, on the other hand, the Generals, Officers, Subalterns, and Soldiers, are in a state of constant activity to maintain the sacred rights of the people:

And whereas, my Proclamation of the 25th Brumaire, of the 7th year, to the people of St. Domingo, was calculated to establish an uniform system of incessant and laborious industry; at the same time that it required from all the Citizens indiscriminately the co-operation of cultivators, soldiers, and civil powers, as necessary for the restoration of St. Domingo: it being therefore my determination that the above-mentioned Proclamation should be carried into full effect, and that the abuses now in practice amongst the labourers should be at an end, from the publication of this present regulation, I do most peremptorily order as follows:

Art. 1. All overseers, drivers, and field-negroes, are bound to observe, with exactness, submission, and obedience, their duty in the same manner as soldiers.

Art. 2. All overseers, drivers, and field-labourers, who will not perform with assiduity the duties required of them, shall be arrested and
                                              punished

punished as severely as soldiers deviating from their duty: after which punishment, if the *offender be an overseer, he shall be enlisted in one of the regiments of the army of St. Domingo:* if a driver, he shall be dismissed from his employment, and placed among the field-negroes, without ever being permitted to act as a driver again : and, if a common labourer, he shall be punished *with the same severity as a private soldier, according to his guilt.*

Art. 3. All field-labourers, men and women, now in a state of idleness, living in towns, villages, and on other plantations than those to which they belong, with an intention to evade work, even those of both sexes, *who have not been employed in field-labour since the revolution,* are required to return immediately to their respective plantations, if, in the course of eight days, from the promulgation of this present regulation, they shall not produce sufficient proof, to the commanding Officers, in the places of their residence, of *their having some useful occupation or means of livelihood;* but it is to be understood, that being a servant, is not to be considered as an useful occupation : in consequence whereof, those amongst the labourers who have quitted their plantations in order to hire themselves, shall return thereto, under the personal responsibility of those with whom they live in that capacity. By the terms, "an useful occupa-

occupation" is meant, what enables a man to pay a contribution to the State.

Art. 4. This measure, indispensable to the public welfare, positively prescribes to all those of either sex that are not labourers, to produce the proofs of their having an occupation or profession sufficient to gain their livelihood, and that they can afford to pay a contribution to the Republic. Otherwise, and in default thereof, all those who shall be found in contravention hereto, shall be instantly arrested, *and if they are found guilty, they shall be drafted into one of the regiments of the army ; if not, they shall be sent to the field, and compelled to work.* This measure, which is strictly enforced, will put a stop to the idle habit of wandering about, since it will oblige every one to be usefully employed.

Art. 5. Parents are earnestly entreated to attend to their duty towards their children, which is, to make them good citizens : for that purpose they must instruct them in good morals, in the Christian religion, and the fear of God : above all, exclusive of this education, they must be brought up in some specific business or profession, to enable them, not only to earn their living, but also to contribute to the expences of the government.

* How different from the former system must be that field labor which is thought preferable to military service ! !

Art.

Art. 6. All persons residing in towns and villages, who shall harbour labourers of either sex, all proprietors or tenants who shall suffer on their plantations labourers belonging to other estates, without immediately making it known to the Commandant of the district, or other military Officers in the places of their residence, shall pay a fine of 2, 3, or 400 livres, according to the abilities of the delinquent: in case of repetition of the offence, they shall pay three times as much; if the fine cannot be levied for want of effects, the offender shall be imprisoned for a month, and, in case of repetition, for three months.

Art. 7. The overseers and drivers of every plantation, shall make it their business to inform the commanding Officer of the district, in regard to the conduct of the labourers under their management: *as well as of those who shall absent themselves from their plantations without a pass: and of those who, residing on the estates, shall refuse to work.* They shall be forced to go to the labour of the field, and if they prove obstinate, they shall be *arrested and carried before the military Commandant, in order to suffer the punishment above prescribed, according to the exigence of the case.*

The military Commandants who shall not inform the Commandants of districts, and these the Generals under whose orders they act, shall be be severely punished, at the discretion of the said Generals.

Art. 8. The Generals commanding the departments, shall henceforth be answerable to me for any neglect in the cultivation of their districts: And when going through the several parishes and departments, I shall percieve any marks of negligence, I shall proceed against those who have tolerated it.

Art. 9. I forbid all military men whatsoever, under the responsibility of the commanding Officers, to suffer any women to remain in the barracks; those excepted that are married to soldiers, as well as those who carry victuals to men confined to their quarters; but these shall not be allowed to remain any time; plantation women are totally excluded. The commanding Officers shall answer for the execution of this Article.

Art. 10. The commandants of the towns, or the officers in the villages, shall not suffer the labourers or field-negroes to spend the Decades in town; they shall also take care that they do not conceal themselves. Such Officers as shall not punctually attend to this order, shall be punished with six days confinement for the first time, a month for the second, and shall be cashiered for the third offence. They shall give information to the commandant of the district, of such labourers as are found in the towns during

ing the Decades, and of the persons at whose houses they were taken up, that the said persons may be condemned to pay the fine imposed by Article 6. of this present regulation. The plantation people, who in such cases be brought before the commandant of the district, shall be sent back to their plantations after receiving the punishment, as above directed by Article 2, with a strong recommendation to the commanding Officer of their quarter, that a watchful eye may be kept on them for the future.

Art. 11. All the Municipal Administrations of St. Domingo are requested to take the wisest measures, together with the Commandants of towns and of the districts, to inform themselves whether those who call themselves domestics, really are so,, observing, that plantation negroes cannot be domestics : any person keeping them in that quality will be liable to pay the abovementioned fine, as well as those who shall detain labourers of either sex for any kind of employment.

Art. 12. All Commissaries of Government in the Municipalities will make it their duty to inform me of all the abuses respecting the execution of this regulation, and to give advice of the same to the Generals of Department.

Art. 13. I command all the Generals of Department, Generals, and other principal officers in the districts, to attend to the execution of
this

this regulation, for which they shall be personally responsible : and I flatter myself that their zeal, in assisting me to restore the public prosperity, will not be momentary; convinced as they must be that Liberty cannot exist without Industry.

This present Regulation shall be printed, read, published, and posted up wherever it is necessary, even on plantations; so that no one may pretend ignorance thereof. It shall likewise be sent to all the Civil and Military Authorities, together with my Proclamation of the 25th Brumaire above mentioned ; which for that purpose shall be re-printed, so that every one may conform strictly to the duties required of him.

Given at Head-quarters, Port Republican, Vendemiaire 20th, ninth year of the French Republic, one and indivisible.

(Signed)   Toussaint L'Ouverture,
                                 General in Chief.

The Author cannot be answerable for the accuracy of the above paper, which bears some marks of incorrect translation. It was published in the *Sun*, and other newspapers, some time in December last, with an introduction, under the signature, "*A Jamaica Planter*," in order to discredit Toussaint's Constitution, which refers to these regulations, and confirms them.

them. The paper certainly, if genuine, proves that *Toussaint* had established, or was endeavouring to introduce a very strict military government; but a man must be grossly ignorant of the nature of West India bondage, not to know that such a government however to English eyes disgusting, is, when compared to domestic slavery, a substitute most ardently to be desired.

POSTSCRIPT.

[218]

POSTSCRIPT.

MARCH 29, 1802.

AT the moment when this work is ready to issue from the press, fresh accounts from St. Domingo officially published in France, are laid before the English Public; and if the information contained in the Advertisement prefixed to these Letters, was not unnecessary to guard the writer from being suspected of disingenuousness, it seems still more requisite now to strengthen that precaution, by requesting the Reader's attention to the date of the present publication; for so fully are some of the most important of his conjectures confirmed by these official papers, that he might otherwise very probably be suspected of having wished to give to speculations founded on known events, a false air of political foresight. Let it therefore be observed that this work is delivered to the Public on the morning after the publication of General Leclerc's and Admiral Villaret's dispatches of February 16, in the London newspapers.

The

The Author desires that these dispatches may be compared with his observations in the first Letter, respecting the probable intentions of the French Government; and that the following passage in Leclerc's Proclamation may be particularly noticed : *" Yesterday their perfidsous intentions were unmasked.— General Toussaint sent me his children with a letter in which he assures me that there was nothing he so much desired as the prosperity of the Colony, and that he was ready to obey all the orders that I should give him. I ordered him to come before me, and gave him my word that I would employ* HIM AS MY LIEUTENANT GENERAL.—He did not reply to this order *further than by phrases that were only designed to gain time.* MY ORDERS FROM THE FRENCH GOVERNMENT ARE, THAT I PROMPTLY RESTORE PROSPERITY AND ABUNDANCE. *If I suffer myself to be amused by crafty and perfidious artifices, the Colony will be the theatre of a long civil war."*

The Reader will observe, that the particular nature of Toussaint's *temporising phrases* and the contents of the letter which he sent by his children to Leclerc, are wholly suppressed; as well as those orders of the French Government, rather than submit to which, this extraordinary man whom the *virtuous* Leclerc calls perfidious, refused the office of second

in

in command, with the rank of Lieutenant
General, and chose to encounter all the perils
of resistance.

Unfortunately, Toussaint cannot state to us
his own case; we must be long content to receive such accounts only from St. Domingo as
the French Government chooses to publish; but
in the mean time let us reflect, that the commu-
nications on both sides were such as the French
General in a Proclamation published in the Colony did not venture to disclose; and let the
words " my *orders are promptly to restore prosperity and abundance*" be compared with their
remarkable context; and with the observations
contained in this work from pages 28 to 42. It
seems to peep out in spight of the address of the
French General, that at least one difference between Toussaint's views and his own orders was,
that the latter contained some specific measures
which Toussaint opposed, for *the prompt restitution* of agriculture. Let any man read the
regulations in the Appendix, and afterwards say
in what means for that purpose the black General would not have been ready to concur, except the restitution of private bondage and the
cart-whip.

Should a doubt still remain on this important
point, let Villaret's letter to the British Admiral
be attended to, " *A powerful force will at last
re-establish*

re-establish in this Colony the form of a go-
vernment prescribed by the laws of the Mother
Country, and protect those principles which can
alone preserve, and upon which reposes, the
common interest of all the European Powers in
their establishments in the Antilles." What are
those principles and that *form of Government*
in the Antilles which are thus identified with
the British policy in those Islands? Surely after
reading this passage, we cannot hesitate to pro-
nounce, that the restitution of the old system in
all its rigour is the direct object of France, and
must abhor the hypocrisy that holds out at the
same moment a guarantee of their freedom to
the Negroes.

It is further to be remarked on these very interesting dispatches, that the Colonists whom
the French Commanders have prevailed upon
to join them, are chiefly mulattoes, who were
presumably free before the Revolution and perhaps have private interests as masters on the side
of the Republic. *Clervaux* who betrayed the
post entrusted to him, is described as a person of
that colour; and seven hundred mulattoes formerly in the service of *Rigaud*, are said to have
sent an offer of their services from Cuba, where
they were in exile. Let it be remembered, that
Rigaud was the zealous enemy of Great Britain, from whose hostility Jamaica was exposed
to great danger till he was subdued by Toussaint.
The

For EU product safety concerns, contact us at Calle de José Abascal, 56–1°,
28003 Madrid, Spain or eugpsr@cambridge.org.

 www.ingramcontent.com/pod-product-compliance
Ingram Content Group UK Ltd.
Pitfield, Milton Keynes, MK11 3LW, UK
UKHW010337140625
459647UK00010B/650